M000282007

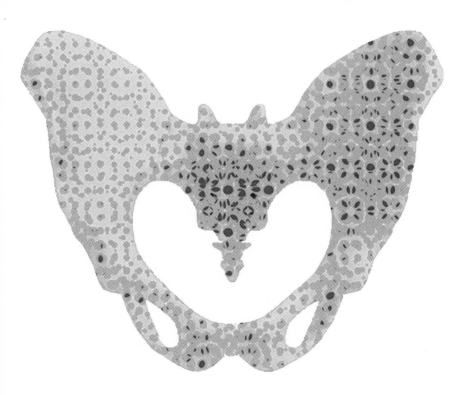

THE SMALL BOOK OF HIP CHECKS

WRITING MATTERS! A series edited by Lauren Berlant, Saidiya Hartman, Erica Rand, and Kathleen Stewart

the small book of hip checks

ON QUEER GENDER, RACE, AND WRITING

erica rand

Duke University Press

Durham and London 2021

© 2021 DUKE UNIVERSITY PRESS
All rights reserved
Printed in the United States of America
on acid-free paper ∞
Designed by Aimee C. Harrison
Typeset in Portrait Text, Century Schoolbook,
and Univers LT Std by Copperline Book Services

Library of Congress Cataloging-in-Publication Data
Names: Rand, Erica, [date] author.
Title: The small book of hip checks : on queer gender,
race, and writing / Erica Rand.
Other titles: Writing matters! (Duke University Press)
Description: Durham : Duke University Press, 2021. | Series:
Writing matters! | Includes index.
Identifiers: LCCN 2020020628 (print)
LCCN 2020020629 (ebook)
ISBN 9781478010487 (hardcover)
ISBN 9781478011484 (paperback)
ISBN 9781478013075 (ebook)
Subjects: LCSH: Gender identity. | Queer theory. | Transgender
people—Identity. | Racism. | Sports—Social aspects. | Popular
culture—Study and teaching. | Creative writing.
Classification: LCC HQ18.55.R363 2021 (print) |
LCC HQ18.55 (ebook) | DDC 305.3—dc23
LC record available at https://lccn.loc.gov/2020020628
LC ebook record available at https://lccn.loc.gov/2020020629

Duke University Press gratefully acknowledges the
Bates Faculty Scholarship Committee and the Bates
Faculty Development Fund, which provided funds
toward the publication of this book.

contents

acknowledgments

I say in the introduction that *Hip Checks* has either no origin story or a thousand. True enough, but it also has two. In 2012, Lauren Berlant invited me to speak in a series on queer experimental writing. I don't think they intended to deliver a hip check with that invitation. But the very idea that I belonged in such a series shifted the way I thought about my writing. It also spun me into writing hell until a talk emerged about my garish pink box. That talk anchors my introduction here—thank you, Annette, for letting me tell my version of our stories—just as Lauren's 2018 invitation to the Soup Is On: Experiment in Critical Practice brought me to the book's last two pieces. In 2013, Paisley Currah and Susan Stryker accepted my odd little submission "Hips" for the inaugural keywords issue of *TSQ: Transgender Studies Quarterly*. That they called it lyrical and welcome in its deviance continued to keep me company as I remained stuck on hips, then realized I was stuck on hip checks and turned that piece into the "Terms of Engagement" section of the introduction.

Other pieces and bits began, improved, and took some unexpected turns as a result of writing and speaking projects undertaken for or with Chelsea Jones, Slava Greenberg, Raffi Sarkissian, Myron Beasley, Jongwoo Jeremy Kim, Chris Reed, Judith

Collard, Chris Brickell, Kirstin Ringelberg, Sarah Wald, Julia Lesage, and Chuck Kleinhans. An extra thank-you to those then graduate students on that list for their under-rewarded labors of organizing and sometimes blunt reminders that the cost of experiment is paid hierarchically. Early versions of writing for *Hip Checks* appeared in the journals *Liminalities* and *Jump Cut* and in the anthologies *Queer Difficulty in Art and Poetry* and *Queer Objects*. I also want to mention as generative the opportunity to present work at Elon University, the annual conferences of American Studies and SCMS (Society for Cinema and Media Studies), and three glorious conferences put on through the University of Arizona Institute for LGBT Studies: Queer Migrations (2014), Somatechnics/Open Embodiments (2015), and Trans* Studies (2016).

Alex Marzano-Lesnevich, Jay Sibara, Rebecca Herzig, Eithne Luibhéid, Carolina González Valencia, Cole Rizki, and Chris Straayer read parts or all of the manuscript, at least once. Their close readings and questions—Who are you as a character in the book? Are you practicing your own politics of citation? Can you find another (s)way?—made a huge difference. So did Duke's two anonymous reviewers. I turned in a manuscript I fancied to be further along than it was; engaging the macro and micro revisions they suggested made the book much better.

At Duke University Press, I thank also Ken Wissoker, who, into our third decade of this, could: act as enthusiastic as I needed him to be about the book that I, but apparently not he, thought I was writing; hang in through some convolutions as I sort of aimed it elsewhere (linear sections of concentric abstraction!); and stay open to the book I figured out I was writing that was not quite what he expected either. Thanks to Josh Tranen for help with many dimensions of manuscript preparation, to project editor Lisl Hampton for amazing and immensely generous support getting from manuscript to book, to Leslie Watkins for thoughtful and meticulous copyediting, to Aimee Harrison for the gorgeous book design, and to workers involved in making books appear for Duke University Press whose labor does not travel with individual recognition. Thanks also to Scott Smiley for another wonderful index.

At Bates, where I teach, the Bates Faculty Development Fund contributed to various aspects of this project, including by funding full-time summer research assistance from Grace Glasson (2013) and Carl Deakins (2018). I cannot overstate their contributions then and later, including Grace's transgenerational attention to the archival 1990s, which productively shifted my vague questions about queer porn of yore toward a tangible silicone object. More students, faculty, and staff than I can name I would like to name here. The Gender and Sexuality Studies Program has been a great institutional home in and from which to make coalition, solidarity, resistance, survival, and joy in times often difficult on campus and off. I am grateful, too, just to start, for my colleagues organizing as tenure ineligible and pretenure faculty and nonexecutive, including hourly, staff, as well as numerous people in and associated with the Africana and American Studies Programs, Outfront, the Office of Intercultural Education, and other groups housed within it, including the students who struggled with me in courses and thesis advising toward more decolonial practices. Since 2012 my thinking, teaching, writing, and life have been greatly enhanced by the chance to participate a lot and teach a little at the University of Oregon, where I presented work at the Center for the Study of Women and Society.

Some of these pieces came into being from my life as a skater and coach in figure skating communities based in Portland, Maine, and Eugene, Oregon. One came from my history as a 25-plus-year volunteer at Outright/Lewiston Auburn. All came about in the context of brutality—geopolitical, gender policing, racist, anti-Black, white supremacist, economic, colonialist, settler colonial, carceral. I wrote *Hip Checks* as a non-trans, white, non-precariously employed Jewish queer femme grateful to work from that position to learn, listen, act, write, and otherwise join in solidarity with people bearing similar, different, and often more embattlements than I.

Not mentioned by name yet but for all of the above and more in work, thinking, organizing, play, family, friends, love, body, salvage, and mighty pleasures: Melinda Plastas, Holly Ewing, Leslie Hill, Sue Houchins, Ian Khara Ellasante, Emily Kane, Geneviève Robert, Denise Begin, Renan Oliveira Ferreira, Therí Pickens, Stephanie Kelley-Romano, Lisa Maurizio, Alison Melnick, Tiffany Salter, Stephanie Pridgeon, Francis Eanes, Raj Saha, Josh Rubin, Anelise Hanson Shrout, Jacqueline Lyon, Paqui López, Charles Nero, AK Wright, Danny Carmona, Yara Abdelhady, Joanne Kalogeras, Nancy Audet, Penny Sargent, KD Diamond, Dan HoSang, Karen Ford, Danielle Seid, Lynn Fujiwara, Sangita Gopal, Priscilla Peña Ovalle, Ellen Scott, Lauren Charles Stewart, Megan Burke, Ernesto Javier Martínez, Michael Hames-García, Danielle Seid, everyone who works at Wandering Goat, Sam Bond's Garage, and Coffee by Design on Diamond Street, Kristin Andrews, Ann Hanson, Elaine Pruett, Shannon Young, Ray Libman, Lynda Hathaway, Vicki Allen, Michelle Doyle, Scott Stackhouse, David Leonard, Anna Kellar, Marilyn and Stretch Graton, Vera and Gary Miller, Chen Si Wei, and many, many Rands, Gratons, Barabases, Suppanzes, Bessettes, Millers, Schankes, and Dorns, Jed Bell, Toby Beauchamp, Jill Posener, Jack Lamon, Hazel Meyer, micha cárdenas, Saidiya Hartman, Katheen Stewart, Jennifer Doyle, Miriam Abelson, Karma Chávez, Lise Kildegaard, Mary Ann Saunders, Samaa Abdurraqib, Daniel Katz, Elizabeth Fertig-Burd, Emma Holder, Kristen Nelson, Nyssa Bishop, Anjali Arondekar, Julia Trippe, Ker Cleary, Anna Schwartz, Sarah Holmes, Gabe Demaine, Wendy Chapkis. I miss you: Dawn Graton, Wickie Stamps, Susan Whitcher Graton, Sallie McCorkle, Chuck Kleinhans, and Scott Miller. Quinn Miller is the reason that "bicoastiality," "unimaginable," and "xoxoxo" are on my autofill; to mix some metaphors in the spirit of our queer ways, those are some bare bones of indelible.

This book is about writing, revising, and being thrown. Life is one thing, and then it's another. I drafted those two sentences before the COVID-19 pandemic and the uprising against anti-Black violence. Revising acknowledgments in May 2020, then June 2020, I could rewrite them daily. Saturdays distributing food with the Presente! Maine Food Brigade. Sunday evenings with the Spark/le Social Distancing the Fuck Up Adult Figure Skater Happy Hour. On the job with the Bates Faculty Staff Solidarity group. In the streets with #BlackLivesMatter and other movements led by BIPOC often queer and trans often young people to dismantle white supremacy, defund the police/militarization/ICE, fight racialized and gendered state and state-sanctioned violence in all forms. Every fucking day more loss, hell, travesty, bigotry, heartbreak, anger, coalition, and fierce love.

Hip Check

AN INTRODUCTION IN FOUR PARTS

 1 · *Terms of Engagement*

HIPS

As racialized and classed markers of gender and sexuality, hips bear weight and meaning, fate and contradiction. Hips contribute to gender expression, attribution, pleasure, policing, frustration, misery, erotics, and joy. Hips occupy a place in the unfortunate system of classification that enshrines hierarchized biological features as the essence of racialized sex. They are called a "secondary sex characteristic" because they likely widen during estrogen-heavy puberties. Hormones appear to shape gender in the bone. Fat accumulations magnify differences. Colloquialisms exaggerate them. Women have hips, we say; men don't. People become pears or apples.

Yet where bone meets fat, supposed biological destiny meets notions of agency and control, of being or having been disciplined. A minute on your lips, forever on your hips: big hips can signal feminine excess or the insufficient restraint of people who are brown, "ethnic," zaftig, poor. It's common wisdom that hips can betray you—reveal who you are or turn on you, sometimes simultaneously. They may swish, switch, or sway as if they couldn't do otherwise, as if queer, femme, or hot mama were essential identities, uncontrollable moving forces. Or maybe they don't do any of those things. My hips just don't move that way, you might say, in despair, pride, or relief.

Hips can seem hopelessly immutable in structure or malleable in shape and meaning, bringing formidable barriers or giddy thrills to projects of self-representation. When it comes to hips, all of the following can matter: the right belt, the right hormone ratios (that you come with or alter); stomach, shoulders, thighs, and butt; muscle, food, training; the uniform, the outfit; spandex, padding; disposable income for all of the above; ideas about essence, affinity, and culture working their way separately or together. What if I told you that I'm a natural with a hula hoop? What's that about? Or not about? The stakes include gender attribution and gendered pleasures. Maybe I want a soft curve or vertical hardness when you put your hands on my hips just so. The wrong hips can be anguish; the right hips divine. Hips don't lie, Shakira says.[1] That depends on what you mean by lying and if you have the resources to make hips speak for you.

HIP CHECK

1 *Point of inspection* Doctors, documents, demeanor. Straight lines and curves mixed up or matched up.

2 *Flirtation device* Notice me. Visual effects, maybe visceral. Occasionally physical: the old bump and grind.

3 *Sports move* Force an opponent off course by knocking them from the side with your hip. As with many moves, the appearance and legality of the hip check depend on the performer, the outfit, the beholder, and the rule book. The hip check can look like a battering ram hurling itself sideways or a tucked-elbow cousin of hands-on-hips sass. It can bespeak professional coaching or street smarts, finesse or brutality, finesse at brutality, calculated maneuvers or unexpected rage. Its force and effect can be spot-on or unpredictable, making cost, reward, and alibi difficult to guarantee.

Hip checks may jar you silently or come with the soundtrack of consequences: Take that! Thud, crash, ba-boom, score, expulsion, applause.

2 · *A Story Where an Origin Story Might Go*

In the early 1990s I received a garish pink box from a woman I came to love, as she came to love me, despite expectations that we wouldn't have anything to talk about. Her name was Leola, and we met because I was dating her daughter Annette. Annette and I came to love each other, too, but when we met, we were hardly aiming for in-laws. Both recuperating from "big stories," as my friend Paqui would put it, we didn't yet have energy for new ones. We did, however, have nicely compatible erotic tastes and a big interest in regularly available sex. We also liked each other a lot and, I think, some emotional comforts associated with having someone in the land of crummy two-by-two norms: a logical recipient of news (a person who, these days, would seem natural to text); a date on occasions when heart or custom called for it in a way we wanted to answer.

Thus, that Thanksgiving, we stopped by Leola's on the way to holiday dinner at the home of Annette's childhood friend Joanne, in Bangor, Maine, where Annette had grown up. Leola still lived there with her second husband John. She'd left her first husband, Annette's father, after accumulating the wherewithal to support herself by selling homemade crafts at flea markets. As Annette told it, her mother spent every spare minute hidden away in a closet-like workspace, sewing a thousand scrunchies or making other objects, like Christmas ornaments with knit balls forming the bodies of cute animals, that Annette had shown me before hiding them away.

I remember wondering aloud before the trip if Leola might give me something like that. Annette laughed: of course not. What would a woman who had raised six kids, whose school bus had been a hay wagon, even have to say to a city-girl dyke professor? As a Jew, too, I was frequently taken as an outsider in Maine—foreign, exotic, maybe not white. Still, I wasn't so sure about Annette's prediction. Strangers tell me things all the time. But when we sat down to a full dinner at 10:30 AM, Leola's response to learning that we'd be heading to someone else's Thanksgiving, and I saw a hunting rifle casually propped next to the dinner table, I did think I had entered foreign territory.

As it turned out, however, Leola had a lot to tell me, particularly about Annette being queer. She'd known Annette was "different" since the age of four, she said, when Annette started refusing to wear dresses. Annette listened in shock. The information about her early gender presentation, though new, didn't surprise her. Annette saw herself as butch from birth. But her mother had never mentioned any such thing. Why would she be telling *me*? Annette was even more astonished to see me holding the pink box when she returned from the car, having gone to fetch some issues of *Our Paper*, a queer newspaper Annette worked on that she'd decided to show her possibly now-interested mom. Through the clear plastic bag that kept the dust off between flea markets, you could see the box in all its glory, bearing seemingly every marker of feminine fanciness that a glue gun might apply: folds of shiny pink material, which had a watercolor or tie-dye effect more visible on the inside; and, on top, lace, ruffles, ribbons, beads, and a glorious plastic flower—open, deep, and equipped for attraction.

It's hard to describe this box without sounding like I'm making fun of it. I'm not, though I distinctly remember trying not to laugh as I showed it to Annette. The morning had been so unpredictable. The box seemed at first a little hilariously over-the-top. Yet I loved it, from no lofty distance, and I knew that it was as extravagant in gesture as in embellishment. Leola had bought her independence dime by dime and still lived modestly. Parting with a labor-intensive item she'd made to sell was a big deal. It was a gift as substantial as our conversations, of which there were more to come—often, on subsequent visits, when she could get me alone. Once, before Leola and John moved to Arizona, she waited until Annette walked off to tell me how much she loved her daughter, even if she didn't always show it because, in her opinion, the other five siblings needed more help and thus attention.

Why did Leola have so much to discuss with me? Maybe I showed up at just the right moment, when Leola finally wanted to acknowledge her queer butch daughter out loud. Maybe telling me the old family stories—the *new* old family stories— constituted a gesture of accepting me as a daughter-in-law. Leola, I think, mistook me for the equivalent of Annette's wife, and why wouldn't she? Annette, who hardly saw or spoke to her mother, had brought me home for the holidays. After this first success, Annette always brought me along. Leola never saw her without me.

Besides, Annette and I had the butch/femme thing going, which can offer the comforting familiarity of paired gender difference, at least to people who don't want to kill you after it signals to them that you're queer. Perceptions of commonality can enhance interactions even when those perceptions are inaccurate. And, really, when are perceptions of other people's genders or relationships—or even our own—exactly right? For instance, I saw Annette and her friend Joanne as two old-style white butches, dressed to hide the feminine curves that their dates had on display and in stylish contradistinction to those no-nonsense, straight white women who can confuse newcomers in states like Maine or Wisconsin, even newcomers like me with seriously refined butchdar. Over Thanksgiving dinner, however, Annette and Joanne talked about how happy they were to have traditional butch/femme roles behind them. Yet despite laughing off those old roles, Annette considered some butch/ femme divisions of labor nonnegotiable and had already developed tricks to scam me, fearing incorrectly—preconceptions again—that they might offend my feminist tendencies. "I'll drive us to Bangor," she had said, "since you drove to my place." She really meant: "The butch always drives." She fooled me on the driving for years until she had a bout of sciatica that required *me* to drive; Annette wanted to duck rather than be seen as the passenger.

Leola and I had girl talk: woman to woman, woman to femme, mother to daughter-in-law. It was all of those simultaneously, none of those exactly, and more than any of those, too. Fundamentally, we really liked each other. Besides, despite our differences, we had a lot in common, including one thing that brought me and Annette together: a big interest in sex. Annette's father told me during our very brief, one-time encounter that Leola had left him because he couldn't satisfy her sexually. I don't know if that was true, but I quite loved the idea. I'd come a bit late myself to the notion that it was OK for sex to matter enough to factor it into staying or going. But even setting aside his unsolicited opinion, Leola's interest was evident and hardly only hetero-marital. Once she told us about how she and John had accidentally parked their RV for the night right next to a cruising spot in the woods frequented by gay men. "What did you do?" I asked, expecting some account of disgust or disapproval, given how shocked she sounded. Nope. "We stayed up all night and watched!" she said excitedly. Like daughter, like mother, on more levels than I would share with her or that I will share with you.

Leola's final revelation to me came on a Thanksgiving three or four years after our first, when Annette and I visited Leola and John in Arizona, as soon as Annette and John had gone to retrieve our luggage. By then, the warmth all around was old news. Our roles were familiar, too. I'd long ago stopped offering to drive. I was awed but not freaked—although Annette was still flabbergasted—when Leola gave me a quilt representing exponentially more labor than the glorious pink box. I felt prepared for whatever Leola would tell me. I wasn't. "Don't tell Annette," she said, "but they found a lump down there." That was Leola's final revelation to me. It wasn't because she was dying imminently— she lived with cancer for another decade. Nor was it because I agreed to keep her secret only long enough for her to gift Annette with a stress-free vacation. Our time was done because Annette and I were done, at least in any way that would make Leola sort of my mother-in-law. Other lovers had come to occupy us, but no one could quite split up me and Leola.

3 · Rethinkings

I like a book with a good origin story, maybe two. But this book has either none or a thousand. It began, and begins, in the middle of rethinking: returning to some topics I've written about before; revisiting scenes that stick with me but also keep changing as I live with them, recount them, write about them, and live with them some more.

Like the scene in the story I just described, where I learned that I had misread Annette and her friend Joanne, who considered traditional butch/femme roles behind them, I told it, a lot like I experienced it, as a story of not-so-consequential misreadings that we all do and that are not always hopelessly embedded. That one gave way over a meal to better understandings that deepened over time, as I learned more about what Annette considered integral to her butchness, which depended on acquiring more familiarity with local knowledges in addition to greater familiarity with her, and as she learned that my feminism did not preclude enjoying butch chivalry.

Significantly, too, in this story, respectful engagement, collaborative learning, and good connections do not always depend on getting things right, and getting things right can occur despite misrecognition and along indirect paths. I didn't show up at Leola's wearing feminine frills. I'm not really that kind of girl. Neither was Leola, as far as I could tell. Yet you know when someone says, "Hey, that's really you," referring to clothing or something else that the speaker perceives to suit you well? Well, that ruffly pink box is really me. More important, it was really us, and it made us an us. It forged and stood for, sort of, what our connection would be about. Nicely, too, the complications of intimacy and connection in my story mess up typical boundaries and barriers, including straight/queer dividing lines. Newish poster slogans like I LOVE MY GAY DAUGHTER don't really tell Leola's and my story when the straight one might be enjoying the spectacle of gay sex.

That version of my story still works for me. But I also now see that scene as marking my own privilege and enduring, sometimes willful, ignorance. I used to think of the contrast between showing and hiding curves primarily in terms of the erotic thrill for me. I loved how two people with so-called womanly hips could look in clothes like differently gendered creatures. I didn't really wonder if people hiding their hips—or showing them—ever wished their bodies were different. I didn't ask if they saw a mismatch between their gender identity and their body. Or about how that mismatch mattered, if it did: that it might be devastating, annoying, no big deal, fun, none of those, or several. That the match or mismatch might depend on the situation and that it might change over time, as mine would come to do several decades later.

Even when I did understand quite a lot, I still sometimes shoved that information away from my consciousness when it was convenient to do so. "Why did you decide to write a book on the meanest topic to ask trans people about?" someone close to me asked, more than once before I really heard it, back when I thought I was writing an entire book about hips. Semi-joking, but not. Hips can create a lot of problems for inhabiting and representing your gender. A trans man who became famous in mainstream media partly for the classic masculine V-shaped torso he had body-built for himself told me that he nonetheless hates his hips. A trans woman who likes her hips just fine recounted her grandmother's warning that she shouldn't expect to look female with those skinny "men's" hips. Never mind that the non-trans grandmother, who had no concern about being misread herself, had hips far from womanly by any measure involving protrusion. Hips bespeak gender bred in the bone, maybe more so than other secondary sex characteristics, as hips are called, because of the component that *is* bone.

Yet like all gender markers ascribed to biology, they require interpretation to function as such and aids to help the interpretation along. A butch standing there flashing a self-fashioned look with just the right deftly chosen pants *is* standing, can stand, can deploy at least some of the normative physical abilities that help to present legible conventions of queer gender. They have marshaled other, perhaps considerable resources to pull that look off, including time, money, learned skills, and comrades in gender, as well as resources to move about in it. Boundary policing can make it difficult or impossible for people who appear gender-nonconforming to venture onto the street, into a public bathroom, through airport security or a day at school. Virtually every day I was writing this book I could have written about a new incident demonstrating the vulnerability to microaggression, hostility, harassment, violence, and death related to being read as gender-nonconforming or trans.

Especially for people read as gender-nonconforming and/or trans and also Black, Brown, Asian, Latinx, and/or Indigenous. Race and racism figure always in the systems of power and oppression that affect gender self-determination, which Eric Stanley well describes as people's ability to "express whatever genders they choose at any given moment," whether they "firmly identify as one or more particular genders . . . [or] have a more shifting relation via their racialized bodies, gendered desires, physical presentations, and the words available to comprehend these intersections."[2] As Stanley also emphasizes, making the space for gender self-determination is a collective political project.

One small measure of the entrenchments that participants in that project confront is the perception and treatment of #BlackLivesMatter (BLM) protestors at LGBT Pride events. Despite having been designated as an Honoured Group by Pride Toronto, members of BLM-Toronto were categorized in both mainstream and mainstream queer media as criminal, terrorist, aggressive outsiders for holding a nonviolent sit-in at the 2016 Pride parade, where they demanded the disinclusion of police in the parade and more resources for Black queer and trans people.[3]

A year later, at the Pride march in Columbus, Ohio, police deployed what Deandra Miles itemized as "pepper spray, bicycles and the fury of anti-blackness" against nonviolent BLM protestors.[4] Miles, who faced felony charges, was among the arrested protestors who became known as #BlackPride4. The Washington, DC, group No Justice No Pride well characterized the implications of what happened to them: "The fact that . . . flimsy, politically-motivated charges even made it to a trial is disturbing, and demonstrates the significant obstacles faced by those seeking to undo the larger LGBT movement's collusion with systems of White supremacy, state violence, and predatory capitalism."[5]

The evidence and effects of racism can be direct or indirect, overt or submerged, always bearing historic traces at various removes from current conditions. The story I told about me, Leola, and Annette took place against a history of hostility to people of French Canadian descent whose ancestors, like Annette's, had immigrated to Maine. That hostility included a period in the 1920s of targeting by the Ku Klux Klan that some people link to contemporary prejudice and that contributed to shifting formulations of whiteness among white-looking people who lived, as all Maine residents do, on stolen Wabanaki lands.[6] *French* remained an ethnic slur, and many remembered discriminatory situations at work and school. Like the subtle distinctions I've mentioned between queer butches and those straight women who might jam your gaydar, racialized distinctions among people now classified as white could take a while to discern, too. Those were affected, and transformed, by such factors as sexuality and class. During the period when Annette and I were dating, anti-gay activists sought to position queer people as a category apart from economically struggling white people—many of whom were queer—arguing that protections from discrimination in the workplace would move straight people to the top of layoff lists. In Lewiston, where I lived, the racialization of French Canadian descendants would change again over the next decade, as several thousand people from Somalia with refugee status resettled in Lewiston. As advocates and foes of their presence sought to make or fight off analogies between contemporary New Mainers and the immigrants from Canada who preceded them, they also, implicitly or explicitly, battled over the latter's hold on whiteness.

Hip Checks performs rereadings and redirections to think about the workings and interworkings of queer gender, race, and writing. The short pieces that make up the book range widely in topic, with three interconnected through lines. Primary among them is the entangled workings of pleasure, regulation, policing, and survival—the way that, for example, as I have started to discuss, the erotic enjoyment of queer gender and the tools we use to identify each other often depend on the types of appraisals frequently involved in policing gender binaries.

A connected through line involves conceptions about how people's outsides show or hide their insides. As many writers in trans studies and activism have noted, trans and gender-nonconforming people are often characterized as deceivers, hiding their gender assigned at birth.[7] Accusatory beliefs about opaque surfaces also fuel racism and white supremacy, as do presumptions that darker skin envelops corrupt or inferior mental and physical insides. "Inscrutable Asians" and "shifty Blacks" are just two of many racialized concepts making their way into discourses, policies, and practices. Besides figuring as bigotry, concerns about how people's outsides show or hide their insides appear in many other forms. These include narratives, many autobiographical, about people wanting their bodies to match their gender identities and a wealth of seemingly innocuous platitudes, such as "we are all the same inside." But what actually goes into ideas about how people's outsides relate to their insides, as if these were stable concepts? What and where are the insides, just to start? Garb covers skin. Skin covers all manner of internals, actual and conceptual: skeletons, organs; teeth, holes; nether regions; heart, soul, mind; identities, truths, delusions; what you have consumed or what has consumed you.

The final through line, which surfaced for me in relation to issues of self-fashioning and surveillance that recur in the other two threads, involves what I have come to call cis-skeletal privilege. By that I mean having a bone structure and supporting physical characteristics such as fat distribution that facilitate the gendered shape you want to present. I use *cis* to signal matching and to gesture to the greater likelihood that nontrans people, who are often referred to as cis, have that match up, although the increasingly common usage of cis and cis privilege has also caused me to hesitate. Finn Enke has observed that these concepts often function to oversimplify both cis and trans.

They may fix people in one or the other position, fail to suggest that the same people may occupy the same position in different ways at different times, and obscure ways that cis status and privilege depend on normative and exalted whiteness, abilities, citizenship, and other matters.[8] So, too, do cisgender identities. As Jian Neo Chen writes, they are stabilized not only "through identification with gender assigned at birth," but also with the differentially accessed and afforded "symbolic and social location provided by this identification."[9] Che Gossett cautions, relatedly, against measuring people in relation to norms of "men" and "women" without attending to the history of those norms. "Terms like 'cisgender,'" they write, "can't really account for how the gender binary was forcibly imposed on black and native people through slavery and settler colonialism."[10]

I work to avoid those pitfalls in one of this book's longer pieces about attempts to identify the remains of people without required documents who, driven to dangerous routes by US operations to deter their entry, die trying to cross into the United States south of Tucson, Arizona. Like all privileges, cis-skeletal privilege is an unearned advantage that can operate whether you are living or dead. People's identities are recorded, tracked, and tracked back through gender. As the generous intention to help return people to their loved ones runs up against the impossibility of gendering people merely from material and human remains, the situation exemplifies how better and worse directions in gendering can collide.

In my pursuit of these topics lies one reason for calling this book *Hip Checks*. I think of the hip check in the three senses articulated at the beginning, drawing on the evocative potential of putting the two words together and the history of the phrase: inspection (hip *check*; hips? check!), flirtation (notice me), and sports move (redirect). Hips are focal points in the understanding and enactment of race, sexuality, and gender, and many of the pieces included in this book involve hip inspection, explicitly or implicitly. Hips themselves, objects that touch hips, and movement involving hips: pelvic bones, shape-forming flesh, so-called men's jeans and women's unitards, hooping, hula, turnout, thrusting.

I also use *hip checks* in the title to signal one of the book's key critical and organizing practices. I pull here from the most common meaning of hip check as a sports move, which I find both imperfectly and superbly suited to my purposes. Being hip-checked knocks you off-balance. If you are moving, it knocks you off course, "re-routing" you as the National Basketball Association (NBA) handbook puts it about that kind of move. Where the hip check grates against my intention is that I am not after the reader as an adversary or competitor. Far from it. I write within a vision of collaborative thinking and strive to approach my engagement with others, in life and writing, from generosity of spirit. Thus my excitement, for example, in found commonalities with Annette's mother Leola, my attention to how people might get things right while getting a lot wrong, and my desire to look from different perspectives, to avoid common critical moves that trounce or diminish others, and to view self-satisfaction or imagined superiority as an occasion to rethink rather than rest.

That's all true. But it's also misleading, at least to the extent that it conjures gentle, rosy sweetness, evacuated of power. When I read it back, it sounds like relationships where no one ever gets pissy or sex where no one's ever on top. That's not me, and it's not this book, which is why I like the hip check. My aim here is both to disrupt your paths of thinking/feeling/movement and to advocate for openness to what being hip-checked might deliver, despite or because of sometimes being painful, because of or despite sometimes being pleasurable. What hip checks don't deliver—unless someone is trying to flatten you, the opposite of my goal—is a fixed destination. I like that, too. Instead of leading you through a directed line of argument, I want to regularize interruption and practices of changing direction.

In coming to these goals, I built on experiments in writing that have occupied me for the past several decades and especially the past five years. I say *experiment* even though it sounds more intentional than what usually occurred. I would embark on a project, like a book chapter or conference presentation, with a traditional plan in mind. Then I'd get stuck. I couldn't write the paragraph where I lay out the topic, thesis, and roadmap: what it's about, what I argue, how I get there. Or the sentence beginning "This talk concerns" or "I argue that" didn't come. Or the introductory anecdote or example had reached five, seven, or fifteen pages with no immediate end in sight.

Eventually, a solution would come to me. I use that syntax, and cliché, deliberately, setting myself up as the recipient rather than the forger of a solution. That's how it generally felt: not like I had crafted an answer, but like it had appeared. Suddenly I'd know that the material in the introduction needed its own chapter. Or it needed a short piece of its own that *chapter* couldn't describe. Or that instead of the fluffy yellow dress stashed in childhood grief that I'd long wanted to write about, I needed to focus on the garish pink box from Leola that the dress brought to mind. One feminine concoction with a giant plastic flower led me nowhere outside myself. The other brought me to complications of queer gender, intimate relations, and improbable connections across seemingly formidable divides.

It usually took misery and, if a deadline loomed, desperation, to understand that I could switch things up, sometimes even in ways that I had switched things up before. I think that's partly because departure from academic conventions raises freighted issues of presentation, inspection, and regulation. Heft versus fluff: Who will you think I am, what will you think of me, will I get a job or lose even a precarious livelihood, if I forego traditional signs of intellectual muscle, like proving an argument, or if I abandon respectable language when I think something else works better? Don't swish. Walk this way. Common displays of doing serious work, besides being steeped in white supremacy and class elitism, often sound like proving you're not a sissy or a girl in a sketchy value system where being either of those things is bad. Against this fraught tradition—which I reinforce and reward every time I plop topic, thesis, roadmap into a grading rubric— I had trouble retraining myself. I kept forgetting what I could do differently. Or I would get hooked on an alternative that worked for one project but not another or for someone else.

Hip Checks shares my effort to make muscle memory of experimentation. It is a product of trying, tweaking, and sometimes abandoning a number of thinking and writing practices—thinking and writing, writing as thinking—focused on alternatives to argumentation and, as the project developed, on revisiting, rethinking, and redirection. The book of super-short pieces shifting direction between them became a book of mostly short pieces that may change direction within them. My idea for stories followed by second takes on them generated, instead, an occasional device. It worked for my story about Annette and Leola. But other tales I had marked for retelling often knocked me sideways as I reworked them, seemingly in several directions at once. Also, initially I was keen on boxed asides but gave them up, one by one, then altogether. They spilled in from the peripheries too often for remaining enclosures to make sense. "Why are some sentences in a box?" to quote one mystified early reader. In addition, as I discuss in more detail later on, the race and gender politics of boxing particular content proved more unwieldy than I had anticipated. Eventually I figured out that I wanted to pursue, model, and, ideally, inspire the embrace of redirection, revisitation, and interruption rather than one choreographic move designed to facilitate them.

To this end, besides including wide-ranging pieces and several more re-presented stories, the book shifts focus, sometimes abruptly, from one piece to the next. If you read from front to back, you will find, for example, a Super Bowl ad with submerged trans content—which itself got hip-checked by a #MeToo accusation—right before a piece about a feminist science fiction writer's embarrassment to be caught wearing men's jeans. I juxtapose them because they think in different ways about assessing audiences for cultural meanings.

But I'd be equally happy if you read around in the book rather than sequentially. A bit further along, a piece about an informal survey of how people my age remember the sex scene that was passed around middle school as "page 27 of *The Godfather!*" revisits cultural interpretation. An essay about lavender dildos of queer yore picks up on two earlier pieces that foreground gendered white supremacy. One concerns the stigmatization of figure skater Debi Thomas for competing in a unitard while Black, thirty years before a version of that stigmatization happened to tennis star Serena Williams. It could be great to have already read that piece, to read it later, or to return to it. Or to head somewhere else: to find other connections between or among pieces, to unearth your own version of page 27, to turn toward other people, objects, or texts entirely before, I hope, coming back for more.

In addition to shifting topics between pieces, I also shift directions within them while working explicitly to rethink common hip-checking analytic moves, such as, "WAIT, but!" That issue emerged for me when a friend, responding to some material in a draft, suggested that my "WAIT, but!" habit, which I had not recognized as a habit, stopped rather than facilitated movement. He asked me, using his own hip metaphor, whether I could "find another (s)way." I discuss throughout *Hip Checks* how both my writing and I have been hip-checked—by feedback, by events, and, eventually, by my own body. Toward the end of drafting the manuscript, hormonal changes related to aging compromised the visibility of the curvy hips that had helped me long ago find butch/femme erotics and made for my relationships with Annette and Leola. I first experienced that shift as the theft of my natural queer gender, despite recognizing full well that nature, itself culturally ascertained as such, does not hand anyone gender. I close the book (almost) with my account of grappling with that disruption of my cis-skeletal complacency. The effects of doing so transformed the whole.

While I see this book as a series of hip checks, I also think of it in terms of hip openers. Hip openers are exercises, stretches, and postures that help you move toward more flexibility against some surmountable and some insurmountable limits, often figuring out which are which in the process. They can help you unstick some habits, turn on your heels, and point your feet in several directions at once. This book invites you to open out from the hips, to look here and then there, to think about things in one way and then another, to take this path and then that, and to think about the directions—directions you take, directions you give, directions you do or do not follow, the times you turn or turn around, and how those change where you go next.

4 · *Edits Out Entered In*

Writing involves editing out. That last sentence started as "Writing involves editing, which includes editing out." I made a mundane change, unremarkable, though *mundane* threatens to obscure the aesthetics, politics, and call to neurotypicality hinted at in many writing directives: clean it up, smooth it out, be precise, don't wander, generate uninterrupted flow. For me, *mundane* also obscures immense satisfaction. I love the kind of editing that's like canceling out in fractions mixed with the old game show *Name That Tune*. I ~~originally~~ thought I needed seven words for that first sentence, but ~~it turned out that~~ I ~~could make that point in~~ needed four ~~words~~!.

I want to tell you about three more substantial deletions. They were substantial not always in size, but in the issues involved and my struggle over them—take out, put back, rewrite, relocate, again, again, again, again later—and because my decisions around them fundamentally shaped what you read.

The first deletion I want to mention is that, despite being highly critical of arcane academic words, I sometimes censored language that better conforms with my ordinary speech habits even when it seemed more precise. For example, I deleted the phrase *fucked-up shit*, which I had used earlier in the introduction as an umbrella term for barriers to gender self-determination. It seemed the perfect term, bringing meanings from the rich histories of the parts and the whole. *Fucked-up* has had broad usage for the messes both out there and inside of you, referencing big structural nightmares and personal problems. *Shit* has such evocative potential that I could go on about it for pages. (Deletion within this tale of deletion: I tried repeatedly to shorthand it here.) Together they beat anything else I could come up with. Conversational or formal, cleaner or cruder, the alternatives seemed less accurate, too wordy, or metaphorically strained.

But even though *fucked-up shit* seemed unbeatable, I abandoned it. I feared losing readers from the get-go, readers who prefer more professional language, take slang or swear words as lazy, or are justifiably wary of being talked down to. Even more, I feared looking like the annoying poser I myself despise, trying to sound younger, more hip (anachronistic slang deliberately chosen), maybe differently raced. I did not want to risk losing you at hello. Later you will come across conjugations of *fucked-up*. By then, I hope, I will have sufficiently enticed you to stick with me. I have some faith in my wiles.

My second deletion: On the way to abandoning all text boxes I deleted one that I started writing about Prince soon after his death on April 21, 2016. I love Prince. When he died, I was a week away from performing a figure skating solo to his cover of Joni Mitchell's "A Case of You." His falsetto queered up the rink each of the hundred-plus times I practiced it. Queering it up is also one reason that Prince's song "If I Was Your Girlfriend" appeared frequently on mixes I played over the rink loudspeakers.

If I wrote about Prince, I could linger with him, offering a memorial tribute, on topic, to someone who had died of chronic hip pain acquired in the service of performing queer gender. The musician Sheila E., for example, long close to Prince, accompanied him on his *Purple Rain* tour in 1981 and later mentioned as one likely source of his pain the way he jumped off of stage risers wearing platform heels.[11] I also liked the idea of finding a visual and textual way to mark the jagged interruptions that seamless writing usually masks. Right here, when I was writing this, Prince died. Of course, "right here" would be a fiction once editing changed what and where "here" had been, but the insertion could make the point. More abstractly, I liked the idea of presenting a text as jagged, as hip-checked, as gender and sexuality can be. They are not always about finding your place on a continuum, to evoke a common metaphor. Ideas, events, and interactions can make or remake your course.

I gave up my text box in progress partly because Prince overspilled it. To begin with, everything I told you needs complicating. Hard landings can hurt you whether you're in heels or not. Stigma and racism can get you even if you have Prince's resources. As Lorraine Berry emphasizes in "Prince Did Not Die from Pain Pills—He Died from Chronic Pain," medicating chronic pain is grossly hampered by the mischaracterization of dependence as addiction and by racism, which contributes to the characterization of unsanctioned drug use in terms of criminality and to race-based disparities in how people respond to the physical pain of others.[12] Jay Sibara calls the assumption that Black people in particular feel less physical pain "a widely documented prejudicial belief about Blacks that has contributed both during and after slavery to labor exploitation, abusive medical experimentation, denial or reduction of disability benefits, under-allocation of pain-management medication, under-diagnosis and treatment for depression, and harsher criminal sentencing compared to that which whites receive, among other likely effects."[13]

In fact, the pelvic region figures prominently in the history of disregarding the pain of Black people, who have often been characterized as superhuman and insufficiently human simultaneously. J. Marion Sims (1813–83), inventor of the speculum and "father of modern gynecology," performed surgical experiments, without anesthesia, on three enslaved Black women, Anarcha, Lucy, and Betsey.[14] In "How to Measure Pain I" from *Patient*, a book of poems situating her own medical ordeals in relation to theirs, Bettina Judd writes: "Can you imagine anything / worse than this? / If the answer is no, ask again."[15] Sims was trying to treat vesicovaginal fistula (VVF), a rupture between the walls of the vagina and urinary tract caused by a huge injury to the soft tissues of the pelvis. As C. Riley Snorton writes, the pelvis, besides being a site for medical experimentation dependent on the condition of chattel slavery, "was also a critical site for producing racial hierarchies among nineteenth-century anatomists and sexologists intent on finding bodily 'proof' of black inferiority."[16] An interest in racial differentiation by pelvis continued well into the twentieth century. It was one component, Sally Markowitz argues, of addressing sexual difference in ways that directly or indirectly naturalize white supremacy.[17]

I also reflected about the possible implications of presenting Prince's death as a break in the dominant flow rather than as part of it. Prince, Michael Jackson, Madonna, and me, I used to say, all born in 1958! Part of the joke was my gross lack of similarity to three pop megastars. But let's slice it another way. Prince, Michael Jackson, Madonna, and me: only the white people live to turn sixty. A text box might appropriately delimit my sadness. But the racial disproportion in death dealing, affecting even two Black men with the riches to evade many harsh effects of racism in the carceral state, is integral content for the book.

Text boxes, at a minimum, visually circumscribe what they highlight. As I reconsidered my plans, I thought about a review of my last book, *Red Nails, Black Skates*, by Angeletta K. M. Gourdine, a professor of African diaspora studies, English, and women's and gender studies. Gourdine found my treatment of race, which I had considered substantial and integral, to be "in essence footnotes."[18] While I don't fully agree with her assessment, the vast distance between her assessment and mine showed me that I had a lot to do both in practicing and in conveying the centrality of race in my work, including attending to the racial politics of form and placement.

The third deletion I want to mention involves a friend's post about being gay/trans/gender-bashed while walking home from a queer bar. I found out the next day on Facebook, where I'd seen their selfie the night before, displaying genderqueer style for a night on the town. Their detailed account, in conjunction with the picture, concerned precisely the pleasure and risk in working your hips to present a gender expression that does not match what your body traditionally signals. My friend gave me permission to write about it and, more importantly, seemed enthusiastic about the prospect. They were actively spreading the word themselves. Besides participating in care shifts while they recuperated, I could help in their project of spreading the word.

But consent and enthusiasm do not guarantee someone's response to the published account. Writing about someone else always risks missing or mistaking the details that matter. For example, I never would have guessed one detail that Annette felt misrepresented by in the draft I showed her of my story about her and Leola. Because I hadn't explicitly described her stowing away her mother's crafts after showing them to me, she thought readers might imagine them out on display. A butch, Annette said, would never decorate with such frilly items. While I could easily, and happily, edit that problem away, I could not thereby control either readers' responses to the text once printed or her own. I can't even always predict how I will respond to what I write about myself, once it's out there, after time passes, when I can more vividly conjure readers, when I can't take it back.

Working my way to this deletion helped me think through other matters that I discuss later in the book about representing violence and oppression. These include the contradictory politics of witnessing, which can both illuminate and exacerbate spectacles of injustice, and the politics of citation. For example, while I could have employed many examples and texts to discuss the entrenchment of racialized obstacles to gender self-determination, I used the protests and analyses by #BlackLives Matter activists around mainstream Pride events. Focusing on resistance to oppression, rather than only subjection to it, and on theory generated within, not just about, resistance—and I do not intend here to separate academics from the streets many of us rise up in—I worked also toward the projects of separating criteria for who has smarts from academic gatekeeping.

I thought a lot as I was writing this book about how to abet expansive life and liveness in the face and exposition of opposing forces. I hope that, as a result of what I took out and put in, you will find life-dealing hip checks here.

If Men Don't Have Hips,
How Can They Hip-Check?

 Subtle testimony to the troublesome issues that hip inspection may elicit lies in the curious absence of the term *hip check* in rule books for sports that regulate them. Hip checks occur in many sports officially or unofficially played as contact sports, including ice hockey, roller derby, and basketball. Commentators from casual to professional talk about hip checks as hip checks, post videos of them, and debate referees' calls about them partly because they involve some subjective judgment. In hockey, for example, the legality of a hip check depends on perceived intention to harm, point of contact, and sexism. A hit below the knees recategorizes what could have been a hip check as illegal clipping. Checking is forbidden for children under twelve and for anyone playing as female, which marks you unequipped to handle checking at any age. In basketball, hip checking is illegal, and the punishment depends on violence and presumed consequences, such as the likely prevention of scoring.

But you won't find *hip check* in the rule books for these sports. This must be partly because broader terms cover them, such as checking or blocking. Yet common notions about who has hips figure in, too. In roller derby, a team scores points when a player called the jammer passes players on the other team. Thus, what constitutes passing requires specifying, just as what constitutes crossing a goal line, like breaking the plane in football, requires specifying in other sports. The Women's Flat Track Derby Association (WFTDA) uses hips to mark passing, defining them in the rule book's glossary as "The laterally-projecting prominence of the pelvis or pelvic region from the waist to the thigh," adding, "The central point of this area determines a pass, regardless of the direction the Skater is facing."[1]

But "laterally projecting prominence" is precisely what men are not supposed to have, either by bone or movement. Maybe gay men reputed to sashay or stars of the dance floor—men, that is, with something allegedly feminine about them or their practices. The default for men who rule in contact sports doesn't include that option. It's always played as surprising when football players excel on *Dancing with the Stars*. They also, however, have top-of-the-line "jock insurance," C. J. Pascoe's term for masculine credentials that can protect your status as heteromasculine if you delve into the feminine realms.[2]

The contradiction between hips as pelvic bones, which men do have, and hips as lateral protrusions, which men supposedly don't have, appears in the NBA rule book through odd inclusions as well as absences. Rule 12 B, section 1(a), covers the hip check. It states: "A player shall not hold, push, charge into, impede the progress of an opponent by extending a hand, arm, leg or knee or by bending the body into a position that is not normal."[3] Note that "not normal" appears as if self-explanatory. It wasn't to me, though once I thought about it, it made plenty of gendered sense. Jutting your hip to the side, standing with one hip out, and switching your hips are feminine- or effeminate-coded gestures linked to flirting, sass, punctuating emphasis, and making a human domestic shelf for a child, basket, or groceries. From that position, men sticking a hip out is not normal.

I suspect a similar logic explains why the NBA and Women's National Basketball Association (WNBA) guidelines show different referee signals for illegal blocking. While the NBA calls for "hands on hips," the WNBA calls for "fists on hips."[4] Perhaps rule makers, accounting for women refs, presumed that women routinely stand with hands on hips, requiring fists for a legible blocking call—kind of like needing a safe word for sexual situations in which "stop" may be part of play.

Conventions for the absence of lateral protrusion carry elements of gendering beyond simply sorting people into binary gender categories of male and female. Consider the use of "boyish hips" to refer to slim-hipped adults perceived as women. If adult men properly have no hips, you might expect that the dominant convention for women would refer to adult men. Yet man-gesturing adjectives travel with connotations unsuitable to the task. *Mannish*, the apparent adult counterpart to *boyish*, functions more as a counterpart to *effeminate*, often functioning to imply queer, dyke, or lesbian in the same way that *effeminate* implies *fag*. *Men's* doesn't work either, I think, because proper men with no hips nonetheless have heft, substance, and width. The term *boyish hips*, in contrast, marks the often-unstated way that size matters as much as shape in judging hips, often to uphold norms of race, sexuality, and class. Slight or slim no-hips, instead of multiplying the masculinity of no-hips, can serve instead to effeminize skinny Asians, fags, Jews, and intellectuals.

Boyish also suggests *childlike*, as if women with boyish hips never mature. If you believe some evolutionary biologists, artists through the ages and people around the world, ranging from plugged-in urbanites to rural farmers, value protruding hips on women, judged by waist-to-hip ratio, as a mark of prime fertility.[5] But properly feminine, properly raced women shouldn't have too much of a good thing either. With big hips, depending on skin color, you might look undisciplined and overindulgent, like someone who eats chips for lunch instead of salad. You might seem asexual, like mammies, or formerly desirable, with middle-aged spread, or hypersexual, excessive even for a little jiggle augmenting athletic tone. Jennifer Lopez, looking at editing done on her 2002 music video "I'm Glad," discovered that editors had shaved down her hips even though she had asked them not to.[6] As Priscilla Peña Ovalle writes, "Lopez's body did not represent the ideal performance of femininity."[7]

2

Showing and Telling

DEBI THOMAS'S UNITARD
AND THE RACING OF THE OBSCENE

 Ideas about how people's outsides show or hide their insides sometimes involve conceptions about showing too much, which depend on numerous variables, including which layers seem to be which. What is inside, under, outside, or on top? Underthings hide private parts. They might seem to reveal more, too—identity, character, tastes—especially if you find panties where you expected boxers, ragged drawers where you expected finery, frills where you expected Victoria without the secret, or just what you expected all along.

People who think they have decoded such internals have never simply revealed them. We always make meanings that we have sometimes largely fabricated. We make meanings as well of exposures and exposers. Your panties are showing: You could be mortified, careless, indecent, or cheeky for letting or making that happen. I could be kind, flirty, or creepy for mentioning it. Who do we think we are?

Who do we think others are? Aristocratically toned white girls can make booty shorts look like ballerina gear. Pale skin, lean muscles, and a classy voice can impart respectability. In contrast, darker skin, bulk or bulges, signs of low-budget or the mean streets: Those can color what counts as "showing your panties" whether you are showing actual panties or not. Perceptions of showing too much involve race, sexuality, gender, and other factors.

Consider the rule in figure skating widely known within the sport as the Debi Thomas rule. From 1989 to 2005, this rule prohibited people competing as "Girls" or "Ladies," to use the official categories, from competing in unitard costumes. The International Skating Union instituted the rule after US skater Thomas, famous as the first Black medalist at any Winter Olympics, wore one for her short program at the 1988 Games.

What made Thomas's unitard inappropriate enough to be retrospectively censured? For context, know that competitive figure skating is bound by an astounding number of rules. In the 2019–20 rule book, the rule that "Ladies may wear skirts, trousers and tights (including unitards)" is number 6033 of the 9923 rules of sport.[1] In figure skating, too, the expectation of constantly flashing panties is built into the standard costume for people competing in female-labeled categories. Most wear a dress with a short flaring skirt that flies up to reveal a matching leotard bottom when the skater jumps, spins, performs a spiral (skating arabesque), skates fast, or sometimes even just moves. The other skater whose costume generated a rule after that Olympics, white German skater Katarina Witt, committed a more obvious offense, though it was disguised in the so-called Katarina rule, which still stands (6031) as a ban on excessive theatricality. Witt wore a tiny partial skirt made of feathers attached to a fancy leotard. Circling around the butt from hip to hip, it exposed a V-arrow to the crotch created by the garment's high-leg cut and highlighted by the white stripes descending diagonally to gather like pubic hair in dense white sparkles.

In a 2009 interview Thomas acted bemused about the nickname and existence of the Debi Thomas rule. Not the first to wear a unitard in high-level competition, she had been inspired by seeing the (white) skater Jill Scott don one at the 1983 US National Figure Skating Championships for a routine skated to music from the musical *Cats*: "She had this fantastic program and it looked great, and that's where I got the idea. I was skating to rock music, Dead or Alive's 'Something in My House,' and it didn't make any sense to wear a skirt." Besides, Thomas added, laughing, the unitard she wore "wasn't too revealing. Wedgies are revealing."[2] Thomas may refer here to figure-skating wedgies, a common decorum- and illusion-busting phenomenon. It is not unusual to see elite skaters in elegant finery skate out to their starting spot (a certain model of gracefulness expensively trained into every stroke), then reach under their skirt to readjust their skating panties, sometimes with jerky, wiggly motions, before taking their opening pose.

I just wrote that Thomas *acted* bemused because I don't presume that Thomas actually wondered "why me?" and put "white" in parentheses because I'm the one, not Thomas, bringing race into the unitard issue. To my knowledge, she never did. I'm not surprised. In public, at least, Thomas remained generally understated about racism in the sport, long after such indelicate accusations might have compromised her scoring in ways she could never prove. Claudia Rankine and Beth Loffreda write, "Racism often does its ugly work by *not* manifesting itself clearly and indisputably, and by undermining one's own ability to feel certain of exactly what forces are in play."[3] The culture and rules of figure skating seem virtually designed for such obfuscation. The varied components of censure combined with built-in subjectivity in scoring—in Thomas's day especially with a flagrantly vague "artistic component" mark—make bias easy to act on and hard to nail down.

For example, some people who thought that judges underscored Thomas believed that her marks reflected displeasure with the unitard. As Ellyn Kestnbaum convincingly argues, however, the score likely also reflected the contemporary pop music she skated to, which only people skating as male were rewarded for then, and the way aspects of the choreography evoked "images of contemporary urban dance derived from African American culture."[4] Witt, by contrast, despite sparkling pube-directed arrows, scored what many considered inflated marks skating to a more traditional medley of Broadway show tunes.

Here is another example of how racism and gender policing are always entangled. As Talia Mae Bettcher argues, the ability and resources to present as gender normative have racialized dimensions.[5] While she is writing about mainstream cisgender ideals, these points also apply to the gender norms that dominate in particular contexts, even such tweaked gender norms as figure skating femininity. Their specificities may be nonnegotiable and, for many, unattainable.

From this angle, I think, Debi Thomas in her unitard hardly had a chance. Skating skirts generally camouflage a racially marked feature that skaters in all skins otherwise display: the large butt and thigh muscles that the sport requires. Stereotypically associated with Black people, they get in the way of the white-European standards of ethereal femininity rewarded in figure skating presentation. A Black woman in a costume that doesn't obscure muscles fails twice to meet those standards, especially since the attribution of strength to Black women specifically often threatens to disqualify them from the category of woman itself. As Kai M. Green writes, "too big, too tough, too strong, too black, too masculine, black women have always had a precarious relationship to the term."[6]

That precarious relationship shows up more baldly later in comments directed at tennis star Serena Williams. As with Thomas, Williams competes in a sport dominated in the women's categories by panty-flashing white athletes rewarded for downplaying their muscles, which in turn helps to secure their hold on femaleness and femininity. Also like Thomas, Williams was censured for competing in an outfit akin to the unitard; in her case it was labeled as a catsuit at the US Open in 2002 and then at the French Open in 2018.

I interrupt my path here—another place where I experimented with text boxes—to mark a writing problem I ran into with this piece that exemplifies how sexism and racism can infiltrate language aiming to support gender self-determination. As I hope you noticed, I sometimes use terms like *female-labeled categories* or *people skating as male* instead of the shorter official designations used in gender-segregated sports. I do so because I want to denaturalize the use of binary gender categories, which is generally presented as an obvious and adequate sorting device for sport. It isn't. It does not account for many factors that confer advantage—think weight, height, hemoglobin, funds for training, nutrition, and equipment, just to start. Nor can it accommodate all participants. Some people can participate only under a label that misgenders them, such as nonbinary people who do not identify as male or female or trans women who have not pursued hormonal interventions required to compete against other women. People judged to have purportedly advantageous intersex characteristics sometimes cannot compete at all.

I was satisfied with this textual strategy to denaturalize binary gender categories, more honestly self-satisfied, until the hip check I sought to deliver hip-checked me in the execution. Too often, I could not apply binary-destabilizing language without appearing to legitimize suspicions that some athletes who *do* identify with a male or female gender-presumed-at-birth cannot legitimately claim it. Where fair play is involved, suspicion falls largely on women, given the common gendering of athleticism itself as masculine, and depends on racism, among other factors. For example, as Katrina Karkazis and Rebecca M. Jordan-Young, building on the work of writers in postcolonial studies such as Brenna Munro, explained in 2018, "Black and brown women from the Global South [are] the exclusive targets of the supposedly new, neutral, and scientific T[estosterone] regulation."[7] That regulation imposes medical intervention as a condition of participation on women athletes who have been deemed, by dubious science, to have unfair levels of natural testosterone.

Serena Williams, while not threatened with expulsion, has been attacked for masculinity and failure to conform to racialized gender norms, which contributed to the accusation and alleged content of showing too much. In discussing the discourse leading up to and surrounding Williams's 2002 catsuit scandal, Jaime Schultz notes that Williams was frequently characterized as being insufficiently or non-female, sometimes distinct from human, and attacked for "exhibiting muscular masculinity." In contrast, a white woman, Anne White, had been judged for "accentuating her feminine assets" and heterosexual appeal when she wore a similar outfit to compete at Wimbledon in 1985.[8]

Thus, to describe Williams as competing in a female-labeled category at best echoes and at worst endorses racist hostility, which persists to this day if more visibly challenged, at least sometimes. In 2018 the president of the French Tennis Federation announced plans to impose a new dress code after Williams competed in the French Open wearing what she called a "Wakanda-inspired catsuit," referencing the fictional African nation in the recently released, primarily Black-cast superhero movie *Black Panther*.[9] Accusations of racism spread widely enough on social media and elsewhere—"The Catsuit Ban against Serena Williams Is Racist, Sexist, and Sizeist AF" as the *Teen Vogue* Daily Newsletter announced—for the accusation itself to become a mainstream news story.[10]

In 2019, however, mainstream commentators on Williams's new French Open outfit generally referred to the 2018 censure without mentioning racism, though her new costume spoke back to it. Its zebra print refuses the anti-Black, anti-human, hypermasculinizing gorilla labels often applied to Williams. The outfit also speaks through the words *Mother, Goddess, Queen,* and *Champion* that appear on it in French and English. *Queen* arguably includes Williams in a pantheon of honored Blackness: Wakanda royalty, Nefertiti, Beyoncé, Janelle Monáe of the song "Q.U.E.E.N.," which announces that "the booty don't lie."[11] *Mother* most certainly gestures to one feature of the catsuit that had made its censure an affront. It had been designed partly for her health, with compression features to discourage the blood clots she had dealt with after giving birth. Several months before the 2018 French Open, Williams had been widely quoted discussing that experience in relation specifically to a continuing history of disregard for the health of Black women and African Americans.[12] Yet by 2019 the health function of the catsuit appeared as an unraced health issue.[13] As with the Debi Thomas rule, the catsuit matter now plays when politicized primarily as an issue of sexism, turning an integral element into a buried layer. Racism, like the bodysuited Black body, may be deemed indecorous to show.

3

Deep into Drivel

A BURGER KING PRIDE STUNT,
MUNDANE RACISM, AND THE RAINBOW

 Beauty is only skin-deep. You're beautiful inside and out. It's what's on the inside that counts. I'm interested in the relationship between the profusion of vague platitudes about whether people's outsides display their insides and assessments tethered to bodily particulars of race, gender, and sexuality. In 2014 Burger King introduced a made-for-viral Pride video that well illustrates the interconnections that may operate among insides/outsides concepts that appear to operate at different levels of depth and toxicity.[1]

The video begins at a franchise along the San Francisco Pride parade route where employees working the counter invite customers to buy a Proud Whopper® instead of the regular one. What could a Proud Whopper be? Since the employees, we see, cannot answer the question, customers have nothing to help them decide besides faith in corporate good feeling. Those who buy the Proud Whopper try to figure out its distinguishing features. Several think they taste something different. Gradually people notice the inside of the rainbow-striped outer wrapper. Initially hidden by the white wrapper directly around the sandwich, it bears the words WE ARE ALL THE SAME INSIDE, one word on each stripe. Aha. Most people noticing the words seem to find Burger King's message easy to understand and to explain. They share it largely by repeating the phrase and gesturing to the unique wrapper. Toward the end, however, a young boy provides a political gloss appropriate to the occasion: "I think this wrapper means that we all have the same rights."

It doesn't take much scrutiny to discern that Burger King put out the Proud Whopper and its video with shallow corporate intentions. Even by the most tepid standard, the Human Rights Campaign (HRC)'s Corporate Equality Index, Burger King scored only 55 percent in 2014, falling especially short for trans employees, who lacked both protection from discrimination and comprehensive medical coverage.[2] By standards beyond the concern of HRC, fast-food LGBT cheerleading can rarely be anything but pink-washing—that is, the use of apparently progressive gender or sexuality policies to camouflage dubious policies on that or other fronts—given labor exploitation and problematic food offerings. No food shaming allowed here, but the menu matters in the context of differential access to vendors with more nutritious alternatives.[3]

In addition, the Proud Whopper sold only briefly, in a location unlikely to cost Burger King many customers, a point implicitly made by the relatively obvious hiring of an actor to portray a stereotypical homophobe who says, "I just don't really believe in the homosexual lifestyle." The imitated redneck southern drawl and the semi-blurring of facial features suggest campy parody, and a questionable derision of the rural south for laughs, rather than the person-on-the-street interviews that other comments suggest and may indicate.

Of course, actual sales don't account for the Proud Whopper's reach. After that, consumers did the work. Social media delivered $21 million worth of free media coverage. People in the biz call it *earned* media, but that's a classic mystification, presenting bounty taken from others as, instead, deserved and labored for. The statistic about $21 million comes from a Burger King video on the Proud Whopper campaign that brags simultaneously about the advertising bonanza and the message. The "Pride wrapper," the narrator tells us, became "a souvenir, a collector's item for sale to the highest bidder, a badge of hope."[4]

All of the above merits noting. But I want to focus here on something else: the sheer mundaneness of white supremacy in this rainbow feel-good production. In a video clearly populated with an eye to racial diversity—to use the popular term for demographic variety frequently presented as a good in itself—emotion and reason are stratified by race, gender, and normativity. The people tearing up and queering it up are primarily people of color. So are those who thought the Whopper tasted different, "like, more, like, sweeter," as one person put it. In contrast, white gender-normative males use proper grammar and analyze instead of feel. These characters include the first decoder, an Einstein-type hippie guy, and the boy with the rights discourse, whose sister disappears as the camera centers on him. Meanwhile, their white dad-figure—I think the ad is representing him as a dad, but I don't presume that people caring for kids are parents—stands out for his decided unqueerness. While the video avoids altogether the leather-wearing, scantily clad revelers who often appear in both pro-queer and homo-hating Pride footage, he clearly occupies a mainstream against even the less far-out margin suggested by the celebrants of color with tank tops and blue hair. Dressed in a striped button-down, short-sleeved shirt with a conservative hairdo, he reeks with the white respectability promoted by people anxious to demonstrate that gays *are* just like everyone else.

I don't presume to guess how many viewers noticed the white-supremacist tilt of the video, though I did notice that otherwise kickass articles about the ad don't mention it.[5] Perhaps it's camouflaged by the conspicuously multiracial cast, which suggests to me how naturalized racialized hierarchy is. I also doubt that anyone making the video thought of the casting as an opportunity to show how qualified white people are to keep ruling, even if Burger King's current web page on "Diversity and Inclusion" protects the company's justification to discover precisely that. Besides cataloging plans to appeal to diverse cus-

SMALL BOOK OF HIP CHECKS

tomers and to pursue diverse suppliers and franchisees, the page describes striving for "true meritocracy, regardless of any protected status."[6]

That's business as usual, and the video presents images as usual. Einstein guys and young white boys already signal *smart*. The dark-skinned customer performing a dramatic double take also fits a popular type. That type is seen, for example, in the reaction GIFs too often used, as Lauren Michele Jackson writes, in the service of "digital minstrelsy," where non-Black people use GIFs that feature Black people reacting intensely to represent their own extreme emotional reactions.[7]

Because so many people in the video fit racial stereotypes, it's hard to discern people who were approached on-site from those who might have been pre-cast or added in. I also wonder how presumptions affected the approach to individual consumers. Interviewers seem to have prompted the white-looking boy to explain the wrapper's message. Did they ask the darker-skinned boy, standing with a possibly Latina mom-figure who felt "proud" and "supported" by the Proud Whopper, what he thought the phrase meant?

I also suspect simply that a tug on the heartstrings is at work in obfuscation. I'm highly vulnerable to such patent manipulation myself. Sometimes I perceive the sketchy politics but weep anyway. Frequently, though, I miss a lot, at least for a while, which I think was the case here. I'm confident that the video never made me think "Burger King rocks!" Yet I don't remember how long I took to notice the raced and gendered assignment of reason and emotion or that the message of the wrapper+slogan does not really map onto queer-friendliness, even bullshit queer friendliness, as easily as the video implies. After all, the rainbow content is the wrapping, not even skin-deep, and praising fundamental similarity hardly suggests respect for the profoundly queer among us. Typically, campaigns to win support for queer people by appealing to universal human characteristics foreground people with the ability and desire to conform to dominant norms. In the language of long-standing disagreement about what constitutes queer liberation, such campaigns favor assimilation rather than anti-assimilation. That white dad-guy could have been hired right out of an ad for "marriage equality."

So much remains speculation about how cultural material conveys meaning, including what it means to whom and when. In addition, as my students constantly point out, cultural products look different after you spend time with them, especially from a mindset to analyze their politics. Still, "we are all the same inside" seems like one of those insides/outsides platitudes exceedingly primed to be charming, maybe because they abound as if self-explanatory.

Corporate Pride gestures that obfuscate racism abound, too. In Portland, Maine, where I live, the PridePortland! steering committee faced outrage in 2018 over a decision to limit promotional materials that businesses could toss to spectators along the parade route. That was part of an attempt to shift the focus of Pride back to grassroots activism and to expand inclusion by centering people previously marginalized from Pride planning and events, including trans and gender-nonconforming people, people of color, older people, and people living with economic struggles, disabilities, and other challenges. One of the corporate sponsors that drew passionate defense was TD Bank, which had also drawn attention recently for contributing to the financing of the Dakota Access Pipeline (DAPL), slated to run through the treaty lands of the Sioux. Rerouted from Bismarck, North Dakota, when predominantly white residents feared an effect on their drinking water, DAPL generated massive resistance at Standing Rock to this episode within the long history of colonizing violence against Indigenous peoples. The HRC Corporate Equality Index, which gave TD Bank a stellar rating that year, includes no concern for the likes of that.

In writing about gender self-determination in the introduction, I quoted a statement by the group No Justice No Pride, which, in responding to the harsh treatment of #BlackLivesMatter protestors at a Pride march, cited "the significant obstacles faced by those seeking to undo the larger LGBT movement's collusion with systems of White supremacy, state violence, and predatory capitalism."[8] I saw those interlocking systems repeatedly in comment threads on social media and at a post-Pride forum I attended.[9] Support for corporate benevolence shared space with perceptions that white gay men had been excluded, rather than decentered, and with a refusal to hear that increased police presence made some people, especially people of color, feel less safe rather than more. One white woman countered that the police chief in her town had attended her lesbian wedding. The hierarchies embedded in the Burger King Pride video repeatedly bared themselves in the claims to entitlements unrecognized or unacknowledged as such.

I want to offer one final proposition about this ad and embedded hierarchies. Besides embedding hierarchies that, I think, stand out once you notice them, the video nicely illustrates a point Mel Y. Chen makes in *Animacies* that our linguistic habits are shot through with much subtler hierarchies of liveness.[10] That is, they register dominant ideas that some people matter more than others, that people matter more than animals, which (or "who" if pets—hierarchy again) matter more than vegetables, than rocks, etc. Here's how I see this hierarchy of liveness at play in the ad: Ordinarily, *Whopper* is accented like *burger*, which would apply had Burger King offered a Pride Whopper instead of a Proud Whopper. If you're steeped in mainstream English and familiar with the corporatized shindig that is Pride, you'd probably inflect it, without thinking, like *Pride party*, because *Pride* refers to the event, not the meat. Or, in burger speak, it's like In-N-Out Burger, where the modifier names the store, or bacon cheeseburger, which describes meat piled on meat. In neither case, for different reasons, does the adjective mess with the liveness of the noun. Turning *pride* into *proud*, however, jiggles the inflection both of *Whopper* and the phrase, which is now accented like *happy camper*, a word combination tacking emotions to a human object.

I think that's one reason why people in the ad sound mystified in asking what a Proud Whopper is. The delivery registers the destabilization of naturalized hierarchies where, ordinarily, creatures who have feelings reside above dead meat. In the video, most of those creatures also reside beneath that white boy with our rights in his mouth.

TV Evidence for the Transgender Tipping Point

 The idea that trans people are characterized, sometimes primarily characterized, by the discrepancy between their outsides and insides—between their appearance and gender identity or between their gender presentation and body—is a notion with a long history marked by big conceptual variations, all layered into contemporary popular understanding. These include, as Eric Plemons details, the idea of being trapped in the wrong body, which was "once the hallmark of transsexual self-narrative," and the "invisible me" discourse.[1] Plemons links the ascent of the second to the marketing of (supposedly) elective medical procedures, only some serving trans embodiment, that burgeoned in the 1990s with ascending neoliberal ideals of self-actualization, privatization, and personal responsibility. In turn, this concept of an inner self waiting to be made visible presages a more recent insistence that a person's gender identity rather than body determines their gender. Thus, people who identify as female are "female bodied," regardless of what they come with. No one is born male or born female, though others likely use the bodies we come with, as well as such cues as the clothes put on us, to presume or assign our gender.[2]

Discourses about bodily or visible discrepancies have fueled various responses, many troubling. The pervasive characterization of trans people as deceivers, hiding their gender assigned at birth, features prominently in anti-trans hostility. As Julia Serano points out, both success and failure can be stigmatized. Success can make people seem supremely deceptive. Failure can make people seem self-deceiving and pathetic.[3] Suspicions of hiding, which may enrage both people who think they can see what's behind surfaces and people who worry that they can't, have been used to legitimate violence. They also naturalize the spectacle-making and invasiveness involved in scrutinizing other people for supposedly hidden truths.

As I discussed in relation to Debi Thomas and Serena Williams (see "Showing and Telling"), ideas about what is, should be, or might be showing or hiding are always racialized. Another example concerns the media coverage of Kye Allums, an African American athlete who came out publicly as trans in fall 2010, before his senior season playing on the women's basketball team at George Washington University. Allums stated explicitly that he wanted to keep playing on that team rather than pursue medical transition in part to keep his athletic scholarship. Yet people kept accusing him of *secretly* wanting to keep his scholarship—thus also making the desire to stay in school look like a dirty secret as opposed to a laudable intention.[4]

How have understandings of showing and hiding fared more recently, during the period that a 2014 *Time* cover story by Katy Steinmetz famously posited as a "transgender tipping point," a definitive turn toward visibility and social justice for trans people?[5] Consider two artifacts of trans representation on US television that first appeared in 2017: an ad for Tide that debuted during Super Bowl LI and an episode from the final season of *The Fosters*, a series broadcast on the Freeform Channel (formerly ABC Family).[6] The ad begins when football commentator Terry Bradshaw, former star quarterback for the Pittsburgh Steelers, leaves his post to deal with a stain on his shirt so noticeable that it's trending globally on social media. In a frantic search for help, Bradshaw runs through a play on the field, busts out of the stadium in a pilfered golf cart, and speeds down the freeway, eventually crashing into the actor Jeffrey Tambor's front lawn. Tambor invites him in and throws Bradshaw's shirt into the wash. They watch TV together while waiting for the shirt to dry. As Bradshaw is leaving, Tambor stops him. "Hey Terry," he says, gesturing at his own chest where Bradshaw's stain had been, which is also, conceptually, over the heart. "It's not what's *on* here that counts. It's what's *in* here." "Really?" Bradshaw asks. Tambor shrugs. "I don't know." Bradshaw returns to the broadcast desk, asks, "Where was I?" to his cohost, and picks up his messy sandwich.

When I saw the ad during the game, it struck me as the first example I'd seen of trans window advertising. I derive the term from gay window advertising, a marketing technique that burgeoned in the 1990s in which marketers incorporated a shout-out to lesbian and gay consumers that they hoped people hostile to those consumers would not notice.[7] Tambor's line about what matters being "in here" not "on here" gestures to Maura Pfefferman, the character he then played on the Amazon series *Transparent* (2014–19). The trans parent signaled by the title, Maura reveals to her three adult children in the first episodes that her gender presentation has been opaque. Despite having presented herself to them as male, looking very much the nerdy male professor type Tambor inhabits in the ad, she is female.[8]

That ad makers could designate transgender so economically underscores how common the insides/outsides device has become as a trans reference. Its appearance in a Super Bowl ad is noteworthy, especially given both the normative and the exaggerated masculinity commonly associated with football, which the ad highlights, too. Bradshaw generates and travels through loud, busy chaos. In contrast, Tambor inhabits a quiet, quiet world where men do laundry, wear spectacles, and watch nature documentaries on peaceful animals while other men watch the Super Bowl. Acknowledging Bradshaw's request to check out the game only with "shhhhhh," Tambor sits riveted by gazelles who move ever so slightly as the barely audible British narrator describes the "extraordinary sight." When Bradshaw asks, "Where was I?" upon returning to the stadium, he says it in the way that usually means "where did I leave off?" But it could also refer to that mystifying world.

Yet the ad also reveals the limited reach of trans window advertising and suggests how shallow and illusory evidence of this so-called tipping point may be. I say this even setting aside the question, unattended in the tipping-point article, about whether visibility is an uncontested goal or necessarily announces advancement against bigotry.[9] I set aside, too, debates about the merits of *Transparent*, including the casting that the Tide ad depends on: hiring a non-trans actor to play Maura. The move was controversial for various reasons. As trans performer and activist Sean Dorsey told me, these reasons include the extreme underemployment of trans women in acting and the image of trans women that results: "I refuse to watch any show or film where a cis 'man in a dress' is representing 'trans' identity. This casting practice is dangerous and harmful to trans women and trans femmes, since it perpetuates the lie that trans women are really just 'men in dresses' [*sic*], a lie that leads cisgender people to mock, fire, harm, and murder trans women and trans femmes."[10]

In addition to these important issues, the Tide ad has other limits. Most egregiously, it caters to trans-hostile as well as trans-friendly viewers who recognize the reference. Tambor's perfect caring-instructor voice could be interpreted as derisive parody instead of a humorous in-joke, especially with the take-back at the end. "Really?" "I don't know." Maybe what you see tells the story after all.

Besides, the interpretation of cultural products depends on the ability or desire to receive cues to invited meanings. How many Super Bowl viewers recognized the reference to *Transparent*? I do not ask based on viewer statistics or presumptions about the size of the crossover audience. People may have known of Maura Pfefferman without watching the show. If they saw the ad at least nine months later—Super Bowl ads have long afterlives online—they might have learned of Tambor's role when he was accused of sexually harassing two trans women involved with the show, including in character as Maura. Whether people who learned about it paid attention, however, is another story. It depends, as has been well argued, on whether they think harassing trans women matters.[11] I definitely could not see Tambor as the nonregular quiet guy or stomach his frequent statements over the years about the "privilege" of playing Maura, after he became one of the regular white guys accused of sexual harassment during the wave of #MeToo accusations.

Contexts of interpretation change. If yours does not include Tambor as Maura, the ad does nothing to help you. While Tambor has a long list of acting credits and awards, including an Emmy for *Transparent*, he is not a mainstream superstar. Viewers might not even interpret him as an actor appearing as himself as opposed to playing a character. By contrast, the ad shows a kid adding a stain to Bradshaw's uniform on his Steelers collector's card, fleshing out the identity of the ad's already famous star. Publicity about the ad doesn't help either. Promotional pieces on the Tide website refer to Tambor as an Emmy winner but not for what.[12] Promotion-generated articles and videos, including a three-part series about making the ad, focus on creating the illusion that Bradshaw gets the stain in real time during the game. No reference to *Transparent* appears.[13]

I have suggested in "Deep into Drivel" that shallow platitudes about how outsides relate to insides can obscure more sinister correlations: "We are all the same inside," the Proud Whopper's wrapper tells us, but, as it happens, the smart people present as white males. With the Tide ad, displaying, hiding, and retracting a pro-trans shout-out all benefit from the device's history as, alternately or simultaneously, deep content and drivel. While writing in front of a *Young and the Restless* episode in 2017, I caught the claim, "At Stouffer's it's what's on the inside that counts," in an ad for frozen lasagna.[14] I'll leave that insides/outsides device for someone else to parse; it takes a convoluted path to the message that Stouffer's uses no preservatives. My own detoured point is that the device's routine use for all manner of content makes it ideal for surreptitious viewer courtship. Tambor's comment can have trans content to viewers equipped with external cues, but it could mean nothing really or something quite different.

For contrast, and to indicate what the broad reach of the insides/outsides device might accomplish, consider a scene from *The Fosters*, a show about a multiracial family in which lesbian moms raise five kids, four originally in foster care.[15] In the episode, which appeared six months after the Super Bowl, 18ish-year-old cis Callie, expecting to start having sex with her trans boyfriend Aaron, consults Cole, a trans character viewers met in a previous season, because she feels ignorant about "what's okay and what's not okay, . . . what [Aaron]'s gonna like and what he's not gonna like" given his transness. Cole's first suggestion boils down to the idea that there are better, more collaborative ways to ascertain if someone wants to remove their clothes rather than simply rip them off. Tacitly addressing a trans partner's possible discomfort with a perceived contrast between what body and clothes signify, this scene bears almost the opposite relation to trans specificity than the Tide ad. The trans reference in the Tide ad is vague enough, and dependent enough on external knowledge, to make trans content, for most viewers, invisible behind generalities. *The Fosters* is trans explicit and admirably thoughtful about attending to possible insides/outsides disjunctures in intimate contexts.

At the same time, representing that advice as specific for trans people misses an opportunity to show that Cole has offered good advice in general. Plenty of people, trans and not, don't want their clothes ripped off, for myriad reasons ranging from aversion or shyness to deep pleasure in keeping clothes on or in having them come off differently. A broader not-only-trans point: Consent involves more than yes or no for acts perceived to turn an encounter into having sex. A broader point still: People differ, which Callie learns when she tries out on Aaron something else that Cole says he likes, having his partner verbally affirm his masculinity. Aaron responds by asking why she's being so chatty. Some guys like that, she's heard. "Not this guy," he replies.

That said, in general the show deliberately avoids portraying trans people as marginal or exotic. One of my favorite parts of this plot begins when Cole asks Callie whether she's thought about what *she* wants. "Huh?" She's never considered it. As both guys emphasize to her, her desires, issues, and history matter, too. Publicity on Callie and Aaron's relationship also reaches for broad applicability. A *TV Guide* piece hailed "the first teenage cisgender and transgender relationship on TV" as groundbreaking partly in its ordinariness. It quotes Elliot Fletcher, who plays Aaron, saying, "In a lot of ways trans people are fetishized or thought of in a weird sexual deviant kind of way. . . . This episode does [a really good job] of showing just how normal and loving this relationship is and it doesn't matter that Callie is cisgender and Aaron is transgender."[16]

I want to separate the underlying point from the glow surrounding "normal" and the stigma attached to "fetishize" and "weird sexual deviants." Fetishes do not necessarily harm or dehumanize. Many of us are happily weird sexual deviants. Normal is a coercive ideal, highly overrated, and frequently obscures anti-conventional elements. When Callie and Aaron do enjoy the physical intimacy that they consider their first time having sex—a judgment call based on conventions regardless of who participates—the event involves candles and a playlist under a waterfall. You could call that textbook romance and/or you could call that public sex. The latter shouldn't need to be muted to destigmatize the people involved. But I do like the show's overall combined impulse to specify and demarginalize, and this example of what a device that travels in and out of trans representation might accomplish.

5

A Lothario
in Gendered Jeans

By the way, you're right about the men's jeans. This is embarrassing but they do fit, and I've bought one pair and want to go get another. And they do have real pockets, and are cheaper. I feel as if all my bones are being broken and reset.
—**JOANNA RUSS,**
LETTER TO MARILYN HACKER,
OCTOBER 20, 1977

 In 1977, Joanna Russ was embarrassed to admit that she wore pants designated as men's jeans. Even privately in a letter to an ex-lover. Even though the jeans fit. Even though they had functional pockets. Even though by buying them Russ sidestepped the infuriating pink tax routinely added to items designated for women. Even though lots of people who identified as women wore men's jeans back then. Even though Russ's science fiction writing, like *The Female Man* (1975), disrupted binaries and slammed traditional limits on women. Even though she's *Joanna Russ*. Feminist icon. My hero.

Joanna Russ changed my life, partly by changing my thinking about porn. In 1979, when *Playboy* came to my campus to recruit for its first "Girls of the Ivy League" pictorial—presented on the cover of the magazine eventually with "Women" shown as an edit in blue-pencil scrawl over Girls[1]—I showed up for the protest without much thought. The chant *"Playboy, Playboy, we're not neurotic-a / No to pornography, yes to erotica"* seemed hilarious primarily for the forced rhyme. I didn't question its premise, that we could or should want to draw a clear line between good (tasteful and artistic) sex pictures and bad (crude and objectifying) ones.

Then I read Russ's essay "Pornography by Women for Women, with Love" in her 1985 collection *Magic Mommas, Trembling Sisters, Puritans and Perverts*.[2] Written long before the internet popularized DIY fan fiction and fanvids, the essay talked about fanzines that, in today's language, "shipped" Kirk and Spock from *Star Trek*. That is, they put them into a sexual/romantic relation*ship* not handed to them by the show's writers. Besides contributing to the growing rumble of hints that an anti-porn stance was not for me, Russ's piece taught me a number of principles that came to underlie my work:

- All people are cultural producers and what they make matters, regardless of whether it acquires elite recognition as art, literature, theater, or criticism.
- Everybody is complicated in interesting ways, including people you might perceive as straight or mainstream.
- People routinely cross gender and other boundaries in sexual fantasies, one of many ways that our sexual fantasies may not reflect what we want to do, or could do, sexually or otherwise.
- If we can't read the meanings or effects of porn from plotlines and surface content, why censor it for that content rather than, say, reject porn made in bad working conditions?
- By extension, paintings, poems, videos, TV shows, the works: We can talk about the meanings we think they invite. But *to whom*? Why do we ever presume to discern the meaning of cultural products by analyzing them apart from the people who encounter them?

I didn't always agree with Russ's particular interpretations, but I loved the framework they came from. I aspired, still aspire, to a practice of critical study marked by the generosity, respect, and nonhierarchical curiosity that I saw in her work. I hope you find that a consistent practice in *Hip Checks*, which to that end has required rethinking and rewriting. I don't have a cutting room floor piled with snark. But it has some, often identified by early readers, along with other excisions resulting from humbling reminders of how much the politics of my writing, and living, remain aspirational. These include several times when, despite writing about white supremacy, I missed its effects on my thinking.

Returning to *Magic Momma* decades later, I saw that I also shared with (or had taken from?) Russ a penchant for using myself as a preliminary case study and that our fantasies could have been dating. In another essay, "Not for Years but for Decades," Russ writes: "By the age of fifteen I was having two kinds of fantasies: either I was an effeminate beautiful, passive man being made love to by another man or I was a strong, independent, able, active, handsome woman disguised as a man (sometimes a knight in armor) who rescued another woman from misery or danger in a medieval world I could not picture very well."[3] I wanted to be that woman she rescued! Part of my departure from (what is oversimplified by the term) anti-porn feminism came from admitting that I fantasized about being some of the women in the nineteenth-century French paintings I expected to analyze for their horrendous sexism in my dissertation, then on "Nude Women and Clothed Men." I didn't want to be in the Orientalist fantasies of Ingres or Delacroix or the nude model that Manet painted sharing a picnic with proto-hipster artists. It was those damsels chained to rocks and such. Sometimes when I reread Russ decades later, I wished for an earlier life as a star-fucker brashly pursuing eminent crushes.

But not after reading Russ's letter to Hacker. Another reason Russ's confession about wearing men's jeans startled me is its abrupt interruption of the letter's primary purpose: to acknowledge what a jerk she'd been. Sorry. Shouldn't have invited you to move here. Don't love you. Didn't love you. Never loved you. Never liked your kid either. Might not even like you now. "But," Russ adds, "that's only saying how shook up and muddled [muddied?] I feel." Small comfort in a litany of characterizations that paint Russ as a lothario chafing against bonds that she imagined Hacker naturally sought. "I felt like a Victorian seducer who'd ended up with a family." "I felt that I had lured you into this situation and trapped myself in it." Those are merely two such gems in Russ's letter.

Hacker was understandably annoyed, taking three months to write back: "I'm tired, I guess, of writing clever responses to letters that say, Sorry I'm So Neurotic That I Treat You Shitty; or I Don't Love You So I Treat You Shitty; or You're So Neurotic That I Treat You Shitty, however brilliantly done." Hacker also addressed Russ's not-quite-honesty about another lover in the picture: "I certainly wouldn't have hit the roof with jealousy. Because, as I'd tried to say before, I wasn't 'in love' either, just trying to work out, and into, a real friendship with a real woman (you) in a woman-identified, lesbian/feminist ... context?"[4] I believe it. Hacker, still legally in a long-open marriage with a gay man, the writer Samuel Delany, was not an obvious candidate for inflexible wifely aspirations. Ugh. Russ sounds like one of those people who think the girl always wants to marry them. Sometimes I think they have hurt me more than anyone.

Then again, I'm imposing. Badly. I used "the girl" in one of its queer vernacular senses to situate Hacker, and myself, as the femme or feminine-roled ones in relation to Russ. Not unrelated to such phrases as "girls' night out" that can have highly straight uses, *girl* may be used queerly in affectionate, exasperated, or affectionate-exasperated ways. Used in a sentence: "Let's grab a beer while the girls shop for yet another pair of hot boots." With "girl," I paint Russ into a masculine erotic role that, it seems, she tried to put behind her. Reading "Not for Years but for Decades" further—a few pages further along, a few times more—I could no longer avoid seeing that the fantasy I embraced is actually dating the fantasy Russ left behind or hoped to. "My most vivid feeling after my first Lesbian experience: that my body was well-put-together, graceful, healthy, fine-feeling, and above all, *female*."[5]

Female doesn't require feminine, but Russ also explains in that essay that she disliked the gender roles in *The Well of Loneliness*, Radclyffe Hall's famous 1928 lesbian novel, in which Stephen, the "invert" main character, dressed in masculine clothes and had begun life skeletally prepared for them, emerging at birth as a "daughter[,] narrow hipped, wide-shouldered."[6] Stephen, that is, has the V-frame associated with what is called "male puberty," although it happens to people of various gender identities who experience particular hormonal changes. Hall's conjuring of that skeleton on a baby "daughter" highlights the deep emotional investment people may have in understanding themselves to be queer from birth.

Russ, it seems, wouldn't have wanted to be my knight in shining armor. Nor, it turns out, did she love "Pornography by Women, for Women" like I did. Archival research, prized for the "finds" it can yield, handed me a big loss when I learned that Russ regretted the essay enough to draft a letter in 1985 to editors who might assign reviewers to the book. While still "believ[ing] that the erotic component" of the K/S fanzines is essential, she wanted to emphasize "a whole range of women's themes: intimacy, the nature of trust, the longing for emotional freedom, worthwhile work, the conflict between work and love, and so on." A later piece on K/S would appear, she said, in a second printing of the book (an edition that, I believe, never happened). "Much less acid in tone (and less embarrassed!)," she writes, it offered a "juster estimate of K/S," in the only fiction she'd ever found, she said, that "is written in Female."[7]

6

Hide and Seek

IN THE AFTERLIVES OF
THE DOROTHY HAMILL HAIRCUT

 When in the introduction I talked about "the entangled workings of pleasure, regulation, policing, and survival," I implied through some of my examples that those categories could be mapped onto an us and a them. Pleasure and survival refer to an us who experience or at least approve of "the erotic enjoyment of queer gender" and use tools of appraisal to "identify each other." Policing and regulation refer to a them at best wrongheaded and at worst deadly. But those divisions aren't so simple. Queer people police each other. Acts of appraisal serve more than one function at the same time or over time. Leola's tale of Annette's childhood refusal to wear a dress must have had varied interpretations and roles before it became a way to bond with me. Motivations for assessment can also be multiple or murky even to the people making them.

For instance, is it hopefulness, survival mode, or snark when my friends and I try to read the hair of a white woman—more precisely someone we presume to identify as white and as a woman—who has a lot of power in our world? We wonder about her gender and sexual identity. Not that we might thereby easily extrapolate friend or foe. Still, it seems like useful information, and to be honest, there is some pleasure in the collective deduction project. Sometimes I think her hair requires it. Sometimes I think it's a dead giveaway. I suspect both are true: Her hair is a dead giveaway because of the particular way that it's mystifying. It reminds me, in its obfuscations, of the Dorothy Hamill haircut that became popular among white women, including a lot of dykes, after Hamill won the gold medal at the 1976 Olympics in Ladies figure skating. If styled just right, the short wedge could enhance the perky white straight-girl look that got Hamill endorsement deals for hair products and shampoo. *People* described it as "swingy, bouncing hair" that "twirls out like a second skirt as she spins."[1]

There's something about likening the haircut to a skating skirt that matches the skating skirt itself: a wisp of feminine signification, betokening modesty, that turns crude and garish once set into motion, flashing panties with every twirl, a crotch shot with every extension. <u>Placing a skirt on someone's head gives them pussy for brains.</u> But stop short of that Surrealist-style substitution, and rest with the twirly good-girl girliness that the authors probably intended to invoke. That's one reading of the Dorothy Hamill haircut and highly suited to the racialized calculus of showing too much that I mentioned in the earlier piece on Debi Thomas (see "Showing and Hiding"). It's the calculus that makes the Black Thomas obscene and downgraded in her unitard, while white Katarina Witt receives stellar marks despite her sparkly come-hither arrow to the mons. Dorothy Hamill fits into the standard white-girl category where routine panty flashing is elevated as a product of a balletic extension that hides the taint of exposure like the emperor's new clothes. Hair twirling out like a skating skirt: how sweet and perky.

Yet the hairstyle's hold on heteronormative femininity could be quite tenuous, as a story by Jo Ann Schneider Farris reveals. A figure skating coach and writer, Schneider Farris was a competitive skater herself during Hamill's era, training, like Hamill, with the Broadmoor Skating Club in Colorado Springs. After Hamill's Olympic victory, her coach directed her to imitate Hamill's cut. Ordinarily, like many skaters there, Schneider

Farris used the services of a nearby hairdresser known as an expert in the style. But one day, when that stylist wasn't available, Schneider Farris "made the mistake" of trusting her hair to someone else. As she recalls, "that stylist, to put it mildly, demolished my hair. Unfortunately, for a short period of time, I looked like a boy."[2]

The moral of that story could have been to stick with your own hairdresser. That's what Hamill did. Her hairdresser for the Olympics was Yusuke Suga, stylist to the stars who also created Donny Osmond's body wave for the 1980 Republican National Convention. Every eight weeks, while traveling with the Ice Capades, Hamill flew him in to touch up her hair.[3] Schneider Farris, presumably, could simply have phoned ahead to confirm that her stylist was available down the road. But that one mishap ruined the Hamill haircut for her altogether. After a Zamboni driver mistook her and her male ice dance partner for "fellas," she decided to grow her hair out.

You can see from the special touch needed to get the feminine gender just right how the Dorothy Hamill haircut could assist people interested in signaling some version of queer gender or, relatedly, queer sexuality at various levels of apparent intention and legibility. Its convenience extended far beyond the wash-and-wear quality that commentary on the style often advertised. Under the right scissors, the Hamill haircut could acquire a queer deviation with a plausible alibi in a well-known (apparently) heterofeminine reference: "I wanted to look like Dorothy Hamill, but oh, no, this happened!" In other words, you could pass off your good hair as bad hair. Good white-girl hair, it's important to say, since the Dorothy Hamill haircut depended on having the non-kinky hair texture associated with racial and ethnic superiority. Good hair has a long history of encoding anti-Black racism. In that sense, it was good hair even when the styling suggested otherwise, as it often did then as well as later. It's not simply fond recognition that generates laughter these days among people who remember sporting or being surrounded by lesbianic Hamill haircuts.

So, too, with the woman I mentioned at the beginning. Femme (of a sort), butch (soft or hard), lesbian, genderqueer: Slightly reshaped by cut or product, her hair might signal one or a combination of those. Instead, it seems deliberately opaque, all the more so when it looks untended, as if to say, "Don't think my hair means anything *about* me because you can see that it doesn't mean anything *to* me."

Does my account of our appraisal suggest hopefulness, snark, or survival mode? The portion of each, I think, has to do with power. It would benefit us to appeal to her. Snark looms when we can't or wish we didn't have to. It's about us being appraised, too, then, which an issue writing this paragraph helped highlight for me. It concerned the sentence "It would benefit us to appeal to her." By the last three words I mean both "ask of her" and "be attractive to her." I was pleased to come upon that phrasing somewhat accidentally. I like its brevity—three words, two meanings!—and how it enhances through layering the connection between power and appraisal in our quest to be fetching supplicants. Yet that layering seemed easy to miss. Should I simply hope you notice, risking that you'd miss it, or explicate it myself, risking that you'd think I'm strutting my cleverness or talking down to you? I picked option three, telling you about the dilemma, which serves one purpose of the book, to bare writing, but could look like a coy, passive-aggressive way to strut my stuff under the guise of a broader purpose. As you see, I fear snark and abandonment depending on how you look upon me.

I return from that writing dilemma to the descendant of the Dorothy Hamill hairdo. Where might I go differently with the generosity of spirit I seek from you and that I strive consistently to embrace? Might I reinterpret *evasive* as openly nonbinary or approach *evasiveness* more openly, especially given my own politics, which caution me not to presume the value of visibility? I imagine that there's more to learn about her desire and circumstances regarding displays of queer gender and sexuality.

7

Consensual
Gender

 I love to spectate consensual gender—gender that people seem to groove on, at the moment or all the time. This includes deliberate displays, splashy or discreet. Especially queer gender: like the way feminine-coded curves can become femme curves as an intentional alternative to a glorious, equally intentional nondisplay of them. But not only queer gender and not always intentionally expressed. I find it delicious in a different way when hips seem to show gender not so deliberately, gender that seems to come naturally and stay comfortably. A few years ago, for example, one of my beginning ice skating students, still working on weight shifting from leg to leg, took immediately to a hip-turning slalom move that her classmates struggled to accomplish. I also like it when hips suggest both at the same time: nature skillfully enhanced. Leslie Feinberg well represents this idea of mastering what you're born with in the 1993 novel *Stone Butch Blues*, a hugely influential novel for many people who came out as trans in the 1990s and a superb example of gender theory presented through fiction. In one early scene, Jess, the main character, walks into a queer bar at age fifteen and recognizes the person Jess has always been in the butches there who will, in turn, teach Jess how to become that person. Here is Jess taking in the sight of Butch Al, who will become Jess's first butch mentor on dress, survival, and, with a "butch 'father to son' talk," sex: "Her body both emerged from her sports coat and was hidden. Curves and creases. Broad back, wide neck. Large breasts bound tight. Folds of white shirt and tie and jacket. Hips concealed."[1]

But as Joanna Russ's response to Marilyn Hacker about wearing men's pants reminds us, it's hard to know exactly when you are spectating consensual gender. Russ's pants fit her but didn't suit her because they visibly signaled men's pants to people who recognized the codes. The pants imposed a gender label that Russ didn't want attached to her body. At least, that's what I'm guessing from the fact that she didn't just utter a 1970s' version of "Fuck yeah!" when Hacker asked if she was wearing men's jeans.

I understand why she didn't. Many people reject garments or accessories that threaten to cloud our gender expression because of their implicit or explicit gender label: a top that buttons the "female" way; a shoulder bag that you do or don't believe is the "man bag" it's marketed as. When you spectate someone's gender expression, you are spectating codes that might or might not be consensual for them and that might or might not be legible to you, to others, or to them.

You are also spectating the interconnected workings of resources, privilege, and ability whether you notice them or not. Numerous obstacles—institutional, social-political, cultural, personal, and bodily—can prevent gender self-fashioning. Unequal access to time, money, mobility, knowledge, and connections can make barriers largely intractable. Return for a minute to the problem of finding the right pants mentioned in the introduction. Let's say that pants are central to your gender expression. Can you find them for sale off-the-rack, interfacing at least sideways with mass-market standards? That's not just an issue of cost, though custom-made clothes can be pricey. Not being able to work mass market, as Jewelle Gomez writes, can hurt the soul and obscure external culprits like sexist, sizeist, ciscentric manufacturers and marketers.[2] What if you need or want to shop brick-and-mortar? Pants that fit are notoriously hard to find. Can you get to a store that will welcome you versus disdain, profile, harass, or humiliate you, a matter that clearly depends on race among many other factors?

Maybe you find the pants you want, which, depending on what you don't already have, may really be the pants you need. When it comes to gender expression, the criteria for *elective* and *essential* should not be gatekept by others. Can you afford to buy them? If you can't now, anytime soon? When you get paid? If you can ever find work? If you skip a movie, meds, or heat? Can you access cheaper alternatives, like a clothing swap, a thrift shop (ideally not the gay-hating Salvation Army), DIY options, or barter?

One more aspect of spectating gender: When you spectate gender, you are also looking at a moving target for other people's interpretations. That's come up already in several earlier pieces: racialized gender judgments about Debi Thomas and Serena Williams; my own fixation, I'm not proud to say, on reading the possible obfuscations of hair; Marilyn Hacker's clocking of her ex-lover's jeans. Examples stand out, but the practice is routine. As Jin Haritaworn nicely puts it, "Biopolitical practices of examination, measurement and classification occur" not only in scientific, governmental, and medical contexts but also in "everyday encounters."[3] In other words, people assess and categorize each other all the time. How we are categorized or mischaracterized, recognized or misrecognized, contributes to how we are treated, regulated, controlled, and harmed.

That is also a lesson of *Stone Butch Blues*. I wrote of Butch Al as Jess's mentor in, among other matters, butch dress and survival. The first contributed mightily to the second, facilitating self-representation, pleasure, and connections—community, erotic, and otherwise. But it also worked against it: foreclosing other forms of pleasure and connection, making Jess a visible target for anti-queer/anti-trans violence, circumscribing access to health care and employment. As Feinberg underscores, access and barriers to gender self-determination depend on specific economic, racial, social, and political contexts. For example, it is the economic recession of the 1970s, rather than recognition or change of gender identity, that induces Jess and some of Jess's friends to pursue hormones and (what we now call) top surgery. They hope that being read as male, instead of as butch, gender ambiguous, or otherwise queer, will help them find work in addition to offering some relief from the type of violence they have already experienced. At the same time, the novel catalogs the type of joys and harms to which gender appraisal had long been integral.

8

Clocking
the Natural

 To projects of movement, as to projects of self-representation, hips can bring formidable barriers, thrilling accomplishment, and hope against hope. I cycle perpetually through all three myself when it comes to one possible effect of hip opening: increasing your ability to rotate your legs away from each other at the hip joint. If you can stand with your heels together and make the toes of your right foot point directly away from those of your left foot at a 180-degree angle, you've achieved ballet first position. Some people can step into it without effort, which in ballet lingo means they have great *turnout*. Some can get there with practice.

Some, like me, can only aspire. I couldn't acquire ballerina turnout even as a kid, when increased flexibility came easier and stayed longer. These days, when turnout would help me with some fancy footwork in figure skating, hip-opening stretches yield a bit of the *ahhh* feeling I attribute to those people who do splits as *preparation* to stretch. But even when I sense progress, I discover by checking my feet on flooring with visible lines that I'm barely turned out to ninety degrees.

It required more fieldwork than I wish it had to extricate myself from my obsession with ballet turnout and learn what an imperfect gift, specialized term, and minimally shared goal it is.[1] A former dancer with natural turnout told me that she deals with painful hip misalignments since she stopped training and has been stiffening up. Derby skaters looked at me blankly if I complimented their turnout at practice—unless they thought I was referring to how many teammates had shown up after a night of partying. No surprise: Ballet turnout ranks no higher than fifth in dictionary definitions of turnout that come up on the web.

Many people seek hip opening with other perks in mind, like avoiding injury, walking without pain, unjamming emotion, releasing stress. A newish yoga practitioner showed me a queer swivel that expanded their repertoire beyond what they identified as a stock butch stiltedness limiting their gender expression. As scholar, yoga practitioner, and yoga teacher Megan Burke explained to me, one potential benefit of hip opening involves the chance to shift "sedimented histories of gendered embodiment" that sometimes suit gendered identities but also may inhibit balance, alignment, movement, and pleasure.[2]

"Sedimented histories of gendered embodiment": limits that seem inherent may have been acquired. Burke's phrase points to one difficulty involved in identifying what comes naturally. There are many. I used to think I was a natural at spinning a hoop around my waist, that I could pick one up at any time, even years after the last time, in heels, flats, or barefoot, and circle thrust it until boredom overtook me. Swiveling my hips, I'd explain, it's a femme thing. Then I learned from trying a super-light juggling hoop that my ability had particular technical requirements. Without the weight of the balls inside the Wham-O shoop shoop hula hoop® I had used since childhood, I couldn't do it.

That was not my first such discovery. Figure skating, another activity I pursue because it suits my femininity—or, more precisely, because I can wrench its conventions to suit my understanding of my femininity—involves repeatedly relearning that what comes to feel natural is highly tech dependent. As the sudden stiltedness that comes with every new pair of blades reminds us, skaters make a million little adjustments, micro-adjusted repeatedly for use, wear, and sharpening, to experience slightly curved pieces of metal as extensions of our feet. But my hooping failure really got to me. It sabotaged a story about intrinsic femme-ness that was painful to lose. I said in the introduction that my body hip-checked my gender while I was writing this book. I'll talk more about that later. But one reason I experienced the change as a blow is relevant here: I began to recognize my femme gender in the late 1980s through a bodily change I took to be telling me something. Until then I had been one of those people who often overpopulate mainstream histories of 1970s' feminism, a white middle-class feminist lesbian who shirked butch and femme identities as patriarchal brainwashing. As my skeptical friend Joanne observed, however, when my girlfriend and I freaked ourselves out by showing up for a party in a tie and dress, respectively, I was a dyke with long nails—"just because it's easier than cutting them!"—dating someone who would never risk the feminine impression long nails convey. My distance from those roles was not as secure as I insisted.

Then my girlfriend and I quit smoking and gained weight in different ways that often get mapped onto gender, like dresses and ties do. Walking down the street with my broader hips and her waist-erasing bigger stomach, we looked like a femme/butch couple, when we had often not even been read as queer before, within several frameworks: to people in the know who recognized butch/femme as a prominent form of lesbian coupling and to people out of the know who expected every sexual/romantic twosome to contain some approximation of a male and a female. Once I realized that the look suited my queerly gendered erotic identity, I started describing that shape shift as nature's way of revealing us to ourselves, or at least me to myself.

It felt like deep truth, though the fact that it wasn't true was never hard to access. Nor later, as I discussed in the introduction, were the hurtfulness and cis-skeletal privilege involved in boasting about an apparently seamless matchup between identity and body. Identities aren't all about being born this way, even if it can feel like that. They are found and made, from inside and outside. I came to see myself as the one in the skirt and changed to fit that picture. As both Mary Gray and Ernesto Javier Martínez emphasize, identity making is a collective project that is not thereby any less personal or authentic.[3] Even perceiving identity as personal or collective involves some socially formed factors. Carlos Ulises Decena explains, for example, that notions of coming out as individual "self-realization" versus the "beginning of a process of social transformation" are shaped by dominant narratives and presumptions of middle- and upper-class, predominantly white gays and lesbians.[4]

Besides, bodily forms, abilities, and tendencies do not make or always match gender. Hips never simply yield up gender—more queer or less, femme, female, or feminine—in the bone, in the flesh, in movement, or on display. Not every femme can or wants to swivel. I don't want to support dubious tests or hierarchies of gender authenticity, queer or otherwise, not least because, as Eli Clare emphasizes, "the mannerisms that help define gender—the ways in which people walk, swing their hips, gesture with their hands, move their mouths and eyes as they talk, take up space with their bodies—are all based upon how nondisabled people move."[5] Matchups confer privilege; they don't constitute proof of identity. Clare writes, too, that valorizing "normal and natural" or "an original state of being" contributes to defining disability as a problem, exalting cure, and manufacturing targets for it.[6] Femme in movement by nature or cultivation: I cannot authenticate myself independently from stigmatization and coercion, especially in this case, where queer and natural overlaps with straight and natural through feminine-coded hips and moves.

Clocking the natural puts you in all sorts of sketchy company. Like with my skating student: When she asked me in wonderment about her sudden prowess in slaloming, I replied, "Maybe you just like to move your hips that way. I do, too." It's true. I do. But I brought myself into it partly to avoid presenting myself, a person with skin color generally categorized as white, as someone who attributes special natural rhythm, body parts, or accentuated sexuality to people like my student with skin color generally categorized as black. Yet even though she laughed in agreement with my hypothesis, and even if we move our hips in the exact same way that feels equally good—natural, second-nature, or happily trained into us—we do so, as Mireille Miller-Young emphasizes, in a context in which Black women have been vilified, fetishized, exploited, and desired in ways different from white women.[7] That includes Jewish women like me who aren't always considered white, regardless of how light-skinned we may be, and who also, in different ways, have been racially characterized and exoticized as dirty and lascivious.

And as for my hoop: Besides helping me concoct an ableist fantasy of innate femme gender out of sedimented histories of gendered embodiment, the hoop bears its own sedimented histories of colonialism, racism, and exoticism with the commercial label that became generic, *hula hoop*. Hula is an indigenous sacred tradition in Hawaii, involving ritual, music, and dance, long simplified and commodified by and for settlers and tourists. "Say the word 'hula,'" Momiala Kamahele writes, "and images of lithe, brown-skinned maidens, swaying, supple hips, and large, inviting eyes beckon one to a romantic sexual liaison sure to bring erotic delight."[8] Naming the toy a hula hoop links the swivel I prized in myself to brown bodies understood to inhabit a sexually inviting primitive elsewhere. Add imperialist export and capitalism: In the first year after introducing the hula hoop in 1958, Wham-O sold one hundred million worldwide, though Japan banned the hoop, reputedly for the indecent movement it would endorse and facilitate.[9]

The company also had free help early on in spreading the word. A US newsclip about the hoop's appeal in Europe used militaristic language of violent cultural takeover to describe the toy "spreading like wildfire in lands already ravaged by rock and roll." The newscaster explains that in West Germany, "from the bourgeois businessman to the bohemian ballerina, the craze hits regardless of class or social status."[10] "The Hula Hoop Song" (not produced by Wham-O), with a little Hawaiian-ish lilt, declares that "everyone can play from three to a hundred and ten" and cautions us to sway, not rock.[11]

The song's characterization of the movement as sway, I think, gestures more to the imagined easy sensuousness of Hawaiian women than to the movement and muscles required to keep the hoop up. It also, thereby, belies the training that can be involved in even the most effortless-looking, or effortless-feeling, hula. What looks natural can mask your training to others. What feels natural can mask your training to yourself. In the 2014 novel *He Mele a Hilo: A Hilo Song*, Ryka Aoki beautifully expresses the way training can evaporate through her description of the gifted Noelani's childhood hula education: "Everything she learned—the music, the history, and the language—seemed to grow within her, until it was impossible to imagine that she ever had to learn it at all."[12]

9

Gifts and Givens

 A friend who read a draft of my introduction liked the way I took multiple passes at a story but thought my order of presentation risked a stifling political correctness. He was talking about my description of reckoning with the way that hips, which I had located in enticing intimate connections, could also be a source of pain and danger, especially to gender-nonconforming people. He suggested that my invocation of someone asking why I had picked "the meanest topic to ask trans people about" served as "a corrective, a disciplinary . . . check on [my] hips/text" that could stop me and readers short more than advancing layered readings. In other words, I was delivering a hip check that prevented rather than redirected further movement.

He'd totally pinpointed a problem that extended beyond my intro. It's my inclination to present multiple passes at a topic as a progression from good to bad, often involving conceptually various conjugations and uses of *fuck up*: WAIT, but! I fucked up, they fucked up, we're fucked up, that's fucked up. "Is there," he asked, "any other (s)way?"[1]

I kept his question in mind—and what a glorious way to put that—as I worked on the manuscript. Revising "Clocking the Natural," for example, I saw that I had repeatedly described joy in movement that feels natural before pointing to the racism and ableism that may contribute to the assessment of naturalness in others or ourselves. So I removed from the end another example of over-attributing natural movement to people of color: movies like *Save the Last Dance* (2001), in which hip-hop dancers of color help white ballerinas, who apparently can't feel the beat despite years of moving to music, come to life and move their hips. Instead, I had *He Mele a Hilo*'s portrayal of Noelani's early education in hula—"grow[ing] within her, until it was impossible to imagine that she ever had to learn it at all"—stand as the final image.

But piecemeal editing doesn't constitute moving "another (s)way." Nor does shunning the role of killjoy when it is warranted. As Sara Ahmed emphasizes, we should not allow derision, such as caricatures of the feminist killjoy, to deter us from pursuing feminist and anti-racist attention and action.[2] So, then, what besides those correctives? I keep looking around for models. For example, how can we address the fraught issues involved in identifying nature, second nature, and training while letting movements breathe that, immediately or eventually, feel just right, maybe natural, maybe destined to do?

I find one great model in the 2014 memoir *Life in Motion: An Unlikely Ballerina* by the dancer Misty Copeland, published the year before Copeland became the first Black prima ballerina of American Ballet Theatre (ABT), founded in 1939. In the book, without announcing it as an explicit topic, Copeland offers a recurring reflection on gifts and givens—the talents she considers innate, the body and mind she came with—that conveys the interplay among fact, perception, interpretation, and the politics of talking about them. Because of both her methods and insights, I share her work in some depth.

By Copeland's own assessment, she had a keen "visual memory," "the ability to see movement and quickly imitate it," arms and legs with "the elasticity of rubber bands," and "rhythmic motion [that] came as naturally to [her] as breathing." It "came ... naturally," but she doesn't mean as a given of brown skin. Copeland plays with notions of racial inheritance in another story. When she choreographed numbers for her siblings, she says, the one with "zero rhythm" got teased that she'd been "dropped into the wrong family or was secretly a white girl in cocoa skin." Nodding to racial stereotypes, the story simultaneously underscores that rhythm is no universal Black trait. Habits of interpreting race vary, too. That was brought home painfully to Copeland when she discerned that her stepfather favored her over the siblings in her "mixed-race clan" who had more features coded African American.[3]

Copeland's gifts, along with countless hours of practice, helped her teach herself and learn from others. She had skeletal givens that she learned to interpret as fortunate through the eyes of Cindy Bradley, her first ballet teacher. Bradley, meanwhile, looked at Copeland's givens through cultural ideals articulated by George Balanchine, the legendary dancer, choreographer, and artistic director of the New York City Ballet, whom Bradley idolized. Through (her interpretation of) his eyes, she could see a future ballerina in a girl with a "small head, sloping shoulders, big feet, and a narrow rib cage." Doing so also required that Bradley could imagine "the brown kids," as Copeland described herself and two classmates, thriving in ballet.[4] This is not to paint Bradley as somehow beyond prejudice. Later troubles involving Copeland's family suggest race-linked patronizing and white saviorism, the notion that white people can rescue people of color from prejudice and harm. But she stands apart notably in a context where skin color routinely disqualified Copeland for ballet to white dance teachers, viewers, and administrators.

Skin color also accentuated Copeland's subsequent deviation from balletic ideals when doctors medically induced puberty with birth control pills. The hormones gave her a "more womanly, physical self" than "the frail-looking white dancers" who predominated at ABT. Those dancers were already better suited by skin to the ethereal ideal promoted by the company and perpetuated partly through costumes "handed down from other dancers with their boylike frames." Like many dance companies with an eye on budget, ABT sewed rigid body standards into costumes used season after season. This practice affects everything from which aspiring young dancers get to perform in their local production of *The Nutcracker*, a Christmas-themed ballet often performed annually with numerous roles for local children, to casting and body-maintenance practices for top-level dancers. Copeland's body thus became a predicament that exposed her to demoralizing instructions to "lengthen," which she calls the legal way to deliver to thin people the message "lose weight." She also began "constantly searching" for undergarments that deemphasized her new voluptuousness while giving her "room to move and breathe."[5]

Copeland's struggle to mask chest protrusions illustrates an important point: The boundaries between masculinities and femininities are messy and formed in context. So are the boundaries between trans and not-trans genders. Copeland was, essentially, binding her chest, an activity often associated with transmasculine body modification, to achieve, instead, a feminine ideal. That feminine ideal, to complicate matters, requires a masculine component, a "boylike frame." Note, too, that hormones associated with so-called female secondary sex characteristics contributed to physical changes ordinarily associated with masculine-coded athleticism. Along with prominent breasts, they brought more visible muscularity, which Copeland linked to her father, a former athlete: "That was where I'd inherited my body structure," she writes, "so much more muscular than Mommy's lithe frame."[6]

Gifts and givens, Copeland's narrative reveals, can be hard to identify, benefit from, and hang on to. Doing each involves gendered and racialized understandings and practices. Copeland "began to notice that [she] very easily built muscle" only after pressure to regain a "lean and classical" line brought bulking up to her attention.[7] Her ability to display that line in ballerina extensions, a display that requires masculine-coded muscle but is often attributed to feminine grace, both characteristics identified through racialized understandings of gender ideals, required that her second ballet teacher, Diane Lauridsen, saw that Copeland's extraordinary flexibility made her especially vulnerable to injury. Lauridsen then drilled her repeatedly on basics to help minimize the risk.[8]

The punishing regime of professional dance changed things, too. So, simply, did living. "As your body ages," Copeland writes, "as the strains and stresses of life become indelible pieces of your being, your dance technique must change as well."[9] Those "strains and stresses" shift your tools for gendered embodiment. Copeland's father, for instance, seemed "shrunken" when she met him in person, compared to the photographs she had seen.[10]

What his strains and stresses were Copeland doesn't elaborate on. We'd need to learn a lot, considering the complex, interconnected contributions to Copeland's own changing raced and gendered embodiments, only some of which I have mentioned. An incomplete catalog of others includes: bodily effects on health, diet, and exercise of Copeland's sometimes challenging living situations and scarce financial resources; childhood idols ranging from her sister Erica (a drill team star) to celebrities like pop singer Mariah Carey and Olympic gymnast Nadia Comăneci, the latter first encountered in a Lifetime TV movie; informal dance opportunities, like "rocking out" to the music of the female hip-hop group Salt-N-Pepa and family favorite, singer George Michael, "post-Wham," the British pop group he first gained fame in for songs like "Wake Me Up before You Go-Go"; immersion in ballet; injuries; medical interventions; and the examples of Black ballet dancers before her, some of whom became mentors.[11]

Notice in this list, maybe, the ingredients of another (s)way, where the problems don't erase rocking out and the need for mentorship doesn't cancel out the connections of mentorship. That's one thing that I'm searching for: keeping the joy in the dance, the pleasure in the connections.

10

Page 27 of *The Godfather* and the Evidence of Memory

 I might be one of those casualties that anti-porn activists warn about, ruined for normalcy by a porn story that fell into my lap when I was an impressionable child. Actually, it wasn't porn by every definition. Not if you believe that the novel it appeared in has "redeeming social importance" or "literary, artistic, political, or scientific value," to borrow the language from two famous US Supreme Court decisions—*Roth v. United States* (1957) and *Miller v. California* (1973)—whose criteria for obscenity made it into common vernacular. Censorship decisions, legal and otherwise, still often rest on them, though an abstract principle is largely irrelevant here. I encountered the scene, at least conceptually, as a stand-alone sex story when *The Godfather*, a novel by Mario Puzo about Italian American mob families, passed from desk to desk in middle school, circa 1970, with the whispered directive "read page 27!"[1] As sex writer, educator, and activist Susie Bright indicates in her memoir *Big Sex Little Death*, kids generally considered the novel itself insignificant. The friend who slipped it to her—same age, same era, two thousand miles west—reacted with surprise when Bright wanted to keep reading: "But there's nothing after page twenty-seven!"[2]

Page 27 anchors one of my sketchier origin stories. Correlation never equals causation, to repeat an oft-repeated truth about deduction, but even if it did, a lot interrupted the path from the text to my tastes. I remember the scene as the one where some important male character (Sonny Corleone) fucks a bridesmaid up against a door until her insides feel like spaghetti. I can connect that to my fondness for certain locations and positions, for being the one in the skirt, for liking sometimes to feel it the next day. But that doesn't describe me until a lot else had happened that I can confidently label transformative, like encountering butch/femme erotics in representations and in person.

Besides, I remember the scene all wrong: the pasta, the people, the circumstances, who started it. In the book, the pussy was like overcooked macaroni, not spaghetti, which I think I had pictured more al dente, as if Sonny's cock functioned a bit like a cheese grater. It belonged to Sonny's wife, Sandra, not Lucy, the woman in the sex scene. Lucy, the maid of honor, had orchestrated her own seduction. Having been humiliated but enlightened in college when her second lover, as unexciting as the first, "had mumbled something about her being 'too big down there,'" she'd been tantalized by Sandra's tales of overuse.[3] I don't remember those details at all, though they grabbed Bright, whose one-sentence summary differs immensely from mine: "On page twenty-seven, this guy Sonny is seduced by a woman whose vagina is so big that only a gargantuan penis can satisfy her."[4]

Page 27 might or might not have contributed to my proclivities. But revisiting it underscored for me a key point about the project of identifying sources of meaning: variations in interpretation and memory compound the difficulty of showing where dominant ideas come from. I'm not taking Bright's account or mine to indicate precisely what either of us took from the scene at the time. Memory is notoriously unreliable. Plus, I can't help but note that we flatter ourselves, and support our censorship politics, in the telling. Two children destined to write enthusiastically about sex, we follow misinformed interpretive paths more hilarious than harmful. For Bright, these included speculation about size: "Did vaginas come in sizes? Did penises come in such different sizes? I had never even considered this whole *size* thing. The tampon I had just used said 'regular' . . . and it was *tiny*. Was the *super* tampon as big as your arm? That's what the book said Sonny's penis was supposed to be like. One of the characters said that it would 'kill' a normal woman."[5] I can't find irrelevant the harmony between our memories and futures.

Nor do I ascribe the difference between our memories to the popular notion that everyone's interpretation is unique. Maybe it's true that, like snowflakes, no two interpretations fail to differ at least a bit. But to me that's no more interesting than anything one might legitimately put after the phrase *throughout history*. Besides, nonidentical is not the same as unique, as broadening my sample of two even a bit underscored.

I posted a query in 2016 to a Facebook group for my high school class and then a Facebook status update more generally, asking people around my age to email or message me if they remembered page 27, telling me what in particular they remember. This was hardly flawless methodology. My sample was extremely limited in number. I knew virtually everyone who responded, even among the 400-plus members of the ETHS 76ers page, which represents less than half the class. Those whose names I recognized were, as far as I knew, white. In addition, several people missed my cue that I wanted their response privately, to avoid coloring the memory of others. Even though subsequent responses were not unduly similar, I wouldn't give myself an A for data collection design.

Still, my sample was enough to confirm that others found the experience of getting and/or reading the scene memorable. One "remember[ed] going to the page very clearly—and nothing at all as to what I read." Another, who got it from a leering seventh-grade classmate she identified by name, offered a full paragraph of remarkably accurate if scrambled detail.

Most memories include one or several elements of Bright's story or mine: a wedding; Sonny and/or a bridesmaid; forceful sex; standing up; a wall or doorway; a big cock, a big vagina, maybe size as a sexual issue. Some responses:

> "Somewhere between rape and rough sex in a stairwell or hallway involving at least one of the members of the wedding party."

> "Did it have anything to do with Sonny Corleone's anatomy?"

> "Does it have to do with Sonny and some woman at his sister's wedding?"

> "Sonny (?) the only one who can satisfy a certain woman because her vagina is so big? Or is that something else I snuck off my grandparents' shelf?"

> "I remember without looking it up that an Italian guy, maybe a groomsman, fucked a maid of honor or the bride herself at her wedding. I think cum ran down her leg. Pretty sure the bride. Pardon my French!"

> "Something about reaching into a bowl of spaghetti and all/whatever that connotes."

That last one, which made me laugh, exemplifies the way our interpretations have variations, commonalities, and rootedness in context. No easy sexual translation of reaching into a bowl of spaghetti comes to me, although we both had some interesting anatomical analogies and misremembered the pasta as spaghetti. I suspect that the latter reflects a period when spaghetti was a commonly served, Italian-coded meal. A famous, long-running commercial for a famous brand of boxed pasta had recently debuted then about Wednesday being "Prince Spaghetti Day" in an Italian neighborhood.[6] It was also, I think, before *pasta* was common vernacular. At least, I remember that when I first heard people throw the word around, when they could have said *spaghetti* or *macaroni*, it seemed snotty and upstart. Now it's more widely generic.

I can also speculate that Lucy's big vagina more likely stood out long-term to kids who read the whole book because it occupies an entire chapter a few hundred pages later. Lucy eventually dates a doctor, Jules Segal, who diagnoses it as a medical problem during their first penis-in-vagina sexual encounter. He then has his surgeon friend tighten her up, tries out the results, and proposes to her. The "strange vagina subplot," as one blogger called it, definitely has some striking features, including jarring shifts in tone.[7] Sometimes the profusion of explanatory detail makes the chapter read like the "very special episode" in a television series that might close with a hotline number for viewers experiencing a character's problem in real life. Sometimes it reads like crude porn. Two paragraphs after Puzo explains that "Repairing the pelvic floor was called perincorrhaphy" (actually perineorrhaphy), he has Jules marvel about his friend "building a new snatch as easily as a carpenter nails together two-by-four studs."[8]

Still, even if my situating speculations are true, so much remains uncertain. When did two of us turn macaroni into spaghetti? On the spot? A week or decades later? What did any of us misread versus misremember? Thus, overall: What are the limits of identifying sources of influence and information without enough information about what they mean to whom and when?

11

Queer
Indirections

 I couldn't stop thinking about the pills in his apartment. The spectacle looked too casual: a fistful scat-
tered across a shallow candy dish with short sides
barely protecting the contents. Like it wouldn't
matter much if someone accidentally sent them flying. Or if visi-
tors helped themselves, knew what they were taking, took one
rather than another, or four rather than two. But it also seemed
too staged. Nothing else in the apartment looked disarranged.

By the time he told me his secret a few hours later, I had already guessed it. He was startled by what tipped me off, which
was what that dish wasn't: one of those Monday-Tuesday-
Wednesday pill organizers that some of my friends had sitting
out, signaling too many pills to keep track of, too important
to forget or mix up. Especially middle-aged gay men like him,
though he had never told me he was gay either. To me the dish
screamed, "These aren't AIDS drugs," which made me fear those
were hidden elsewhere. In a drawer, in a medicine cabinet, or, if
he had been lucky so far, in the future.

I had three stories planned for this book early on. They had
already spent several decades in my repertoire of often-told tales
as examples of sideways thinking that sometimes provides queer
yields. The first one, above, happened to me. The others, which

I encountered, relate to each other as fictional and nonfictional accounts of people outed by their beverages.

The fictional version comes from the late 1980s cult movie *Heathers*.[1] A teenage duo in the early stages of romance schemes to punish two sexual-harasser, presumably straight, football players by staging their deaths as the double suicide of gay lovers. (Actually Veronica, smitten with her demented avenger, believes the deaths will be fake, too, but that's a longer story.) She writes a suicide note about jocks too ashamed to "reveal [their] forbidden love to an uncaring and un-understanding world." JD assembles "homosexual artifacts" to place at the scene. Aside from the "issue of *Stud Puppy*," they suggest irregular sexual tastes and queer gender more indirectly: "Candy dish. Joan Crawford postcard. Let's see, some mascara. All right. And here's the one perfecto thing I picked up. Mineral water." When Veronica suggests that mineral water has become too mundane to signal *queer* anymore—"Oh, come on, a lot of people drink mineral water; it's come a long way"—JD replies, "Yeah, but this is Ohio. I mean, if you don't have a brewski in your hand you might as well be wearing a dress." Sure enough, it is the mineral water that first grabs the attention of the cops who come to the scene: "My god, suicide. Why?" asks one. The other picks up the mineral water: "Does this answer your question?" "Oh man! They were fags?" Even the kids' families buy it. At a joint funeral, where the players lie in open caskets side by side, dressed in their football uniforms and holding footballs, one of the fathers proclaims that his fatherly love endures anyway.

I heard the other story from a new friend soon after I moved from Chicago to Maine for a job in 1990. Recently out to his family, divorced from his wife, and departed from his household, he had wanted to avoid causing more upheaval for his kids. He told them he would be discreet; they could tell their friends when, if ever, they wanted to. I think he imagined avoiding swish, gay pride marches, holding hands in public if he ever got a boyfriend. But when his son confided to his girlfriend, it turned out the kids at school already knew. Someone had spotted my friend at

Dunkin' Donuts one night, buying whole bean coffee. The whole beans were merely part of what tipped them off. It was also that he was buying his own provisions. In their experience, fathers who left usually did so for a younger woman. Had that been the case, surely the new wife would have been buying the coffee.

When I first planned to use these stories in *Hip Checks*, I thought I knew what they were about. Then, in 2015, I started to write them down, using an invitation to contribute to a themed issue of *Liminalities* on contemplation as an occasion to draft some material for the book. I planned simply to assemble them for the reader's pleasure like a string of smooth, pretty beads, presenting thinking already done in narratives polished through repetition.[2] But when I began to transfer oral narratives to text, I started to see them differently.

For example, I sometimes tell that first story when I think I have pulled off another, similar feat of reasoning. I sense a telling absence, an odd presence, a shift in rhythm or timing, a sign of something it has no direct reason to signal. I flatter myself that I have a special gift. Maybe I do. Yet when I first wrote this story down, I discovered during editing that my assessment, and my credibility, depended on certain elisions and omissions. Twenty-plus years later I couldn't confidently place the candy dish. I first wrote *on the kitchen counter*, where I saw it vividly. But as I worked over the text for word choice, order, cadence, and the like, I started picturing it on the coffee table. I saw it differently shaped, too, for a while, then not. Instead of sharing my uncertainty I deleted any reference to its shape and the surface it sat on, thereby also chasing away a nagging observation that in writing as recording I had found memory as revision.

My deductions aren't as mysterious as I can make them sound either. That candy-dish diagnosis had a lot of generating context. It was 1995. Gay men delivered that news too frequently back then. I'd long associated my friend with conspicuous non-information. Also, drugs for HIV- and AIDS-related illnesses occupied my mind and my apartment. As part of a local underground redistribution project to recycle meds to people who couldn't afford them, I'd recently taken possession of our stash to subvert a pending police raid.

Habits of indirect deduction are honed and hampered in specific geopolitical, social, cultural, and historical contexts. My three stories took place or appeared within a seven-year span in locations marked by their own particular mixes of queer activism and secrecy, support and censure, sharing commonalities across expected but not always realized differences between big cities and smallish towns, urban centers and flyover states. The big-picture historical specificities scream out in the contrast between the funeral scene in *Heathers* and its 2013 reimagining in *Heathers: The Musical.* The movie plays one father's newfound not-so-much awareness for ridicule. Snookered into believing his son is "a pansy" and "homosexual," as he puts it, he looks and sounds ignorant as he places the football onto his son's chest, weepily proclaiming, "I love my dead gay son!" The musical turns that line, by then a classic, into a song where the dad imagines a future of PFLAG-type activism, admonishes the more slowly converted dad to remember a certain hot fishing trip in their own past, and, presumably like the audience, has an arsenal of knowing references to gay signifiers like disco, rhinestones, Judy Garland, and bear cubs.[3]

I was new to town when I heard about my friend's coffee. Five years later, in a terrible token of the film's sometimes accurate aim, a local gay high school football star did kill himself (and was buried with his football jersey, too). By then, I had learned a lot more about where I lived than the reputation of whole beans. I shopped at one local bookstore with a gay and lesbian section and another with a covert trail to the goods—one employee's "staff picks" placed by books with queer content shelved in disparate sections around the store. I'd been through an anti-gay referendum that had recently passed by a devastating margin, joining a sizable and homegrown opposition. The combination of in-and-out was familiar enough to me from my previous time in a land of mundane mineral water that I can't parse out the imported in what made me think, "Oh, no, that kid is gay and killed himself," when I read that he was missing—or when they found him after a week of hunting and the local paper, it seemed, abruptly stopped speculating.

I tapped more into local knowledges a year later during planning meetings to revive a queer youth group in the wake of his death. High school kids around the state knew why he had killed himself, one of them told us, as did "everyone who knew a cop." So did the guidance counselor who let queer kids hide their journals in her office and the straight-but-not-narrow activist whose young child longed for pink shoes but had already figured out that only girl-labeled children could safely wear them to school. Sometimes people brought up evidence to back up common knowledge. There was a note, some said. Maybe or definitely it implicated his father's rage. The authorities hid it—out of respect or shame, depending on the account.

More familiarity with where I lived gave me the tools to interpret my friend's story differently, though it took me too long to do so. When I first heard the story I thought, wow, the writers of *Heathers* really nailed it. Here was a nonfictional story about uncultivated hicks who view homegrown gays as urbane-aspiring outsiders and can't even recognize what would count as fancy taste. Seriously, Dunkin' Donuts? But you can also see a story about local smarts grown in particular circumstances, manifest in this one micro intersection of cachet and capitalism. After all, 1990-ish is not like today, when the local supermarket carries Peet's coffee, known back then primarily to people with a link to California sophisticates. The ability to discern dominant social arrangements, beliefs, and values can be crucial for connection and, sometimes, survival. Maybe that kid at the Dunk was bracing for their own family breakup or was queer themselves.

Regardless, their accurate conclusion suggests adeptly mobilized local knowledges. As Miriam J. Abelson suggests in the ethnography *Men in Place: Trans Masculinity, Race, and Sexuality in America*, their accuracy is not always best predicted by proximity to the cosmopolitan. Some trans men Abelson interviewed found their gender more legible after they left urban queer meccas like San Francisco, where people with expansive understandings of female masculinities often misgendered them. Once relocated to the rural southeast, for example, "Wesley" conformed enough to "white heterosexual working-class masculinities" that a neighbor who saw him mowing the lawn shirtless, prior to chest reconstruction, thought he had an unfortunate glandular problem rather than large, female-designating breasts.[4]

I found further perspective on these three stories I have long put together when I encountered a fourth much more recently, called "When Something Is Not Right," in which Ryka Aoki describes a 2008 encounter when she and her friends had been wildly misread. Walking down a hotel hallway with three other performers from the Tranny Roadshow, "a barnstorming transsexualgenderqueer vaudeville show/gender symposium coming soon to a liberal arts college near you,"[5] the group runs across another foursome, who look to be drunk, straight, non-trans locals: two dolled-up women hooking up with two muscled younger guys who remind Aoki of some "carnivorous wrecking balls" she's known. Just as Aoki's group is walking by, "the blonde" yells, "Hold on! . . . *Something is not right!*" and grabs Aoki's arm. Aoki's group fears that she's identified them as targets for queer- or trans-bashing. They discover, however, that, partly by misgendering Kelly, the blonde thinks she sees three straight guys planning to rape Aoki. She refuses to let Aoki go until she's satisfied that Aoki might not be in danger but tells her where to find them just in case.

Finally, Aoki and her friends escape:

We walk down the hallway, and once we turn the corner, we giggle like idiots and dash to our room and bolt the door.

"Okay, now how many ways did they get *that* wrong?!"

Kelly and I are screaming "Oh my God! We fucking almost *died!*" . . .

I flop on my bed and stare at the ceiling. What the hell? And as I finally catch my breath, an even weirder thought comes to mind: In Greensboro, North Carolina, some straight white women, who obviously had other things going on, noticed what they thought was a vulnerable Asian girl from out of town and decided they were going to help.[6]

My plan to record and deliver my stories fell apart for various reasons. These include some that apply to passing along any story, like the vagaries of memory and the way that objects of contemplation, like these stories I considered to be in the can, don't stand still, despite what common associations of contemplation with stillness might suggest. But they also include noticing some far-from-queer elements, including habits of thinking that I was surprised and ashamed to discern. As I mentioned (in "A Lothario in Gendered Jeans") about my early engagements with Joanna Russ's essay on sex writing in fanzines, I have long considered it a central principle to be wary of oversimplifying the complexity and smarts of other people. Everybody thinks and theorizes, not just professional critics or people at fancy colleges like the one where I teach. I also like to think that I dropped the urban chauvinism soon after moving to Maine.

Yet until I sat with this material, I aligned those kids judging whole-bean coffee with the foolish, straight, and fictional hicks in *Heathers* instead of thinking that I might associate at least some of them with my friend who explained to me a few years later that he had to stop drinking diet soda in public because his hold on being read as male remained somewhat precarious. Beverages *can* tell the story, depending on local knowledges that factor into assessments of gender and sexuality.

Aoki's group did some misreading, too, in ways they recognized and probably, because we all do it, in ways they didn't. I wonder, for instance, about Aoki's description of the two women having "bagged two big young[er] bucks."[7] To me, from the vantage point of far from young, that smacks of cougar stereotypes in which older women function as desiring predators, unequipped ever to move the action forward as objects of desire. Maybe those young bucks had at least equally bagged them and couldn't believe their good fortune.

Looking at my own reinterpreted stories along with Aoki's, I see also something I talked about in the introduction when I described forging an important relationship with Leola, who had misconstrued me as her queer daughter-in-law. A premium on getting things right, or a narrow view of what constitutes that, can be extremely limiting. People who thought they knew about a suicide note from a gay teen worked to build a youth group that the region needed whether or not that note actually existed or that particular young person needed the group. The neighbor in Abelson's research who mistook the source of Wesley's chest protrusions recognized Wesley's gender just as Wesley wanted to be recognized. The woman who misidentified Aoki and her friends nonetheless grabbed Aoki's arm "for the right reasons," to borrow a phrase used constantly on *The Bachelor* franchise TV shows to mark the importance of motivation as sometimes distinct from what appears to be happening. While some thinking I considered queer was not queer in the least, queer connections may happen when you don't expect them.

12

Clocking the Unnatural

ON THE HISTORY OF THE LAVENDER DILDO

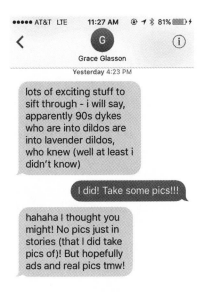

In 2017 a small research project in progress got hip-checked by the text exchange reproduced here. Here's where the project started: I'd been hearing rumblings among lesbians, dykes, queer women, and other queerly gendered people of a certain age that sex and porn are different these days, more cock involved. Actually, I'd heard them among people of various certain ages, with the cock-centric always taken to be younger. "What's wrong with fingers?!" a thirty-ish genderqueer butch recounted lamenting with a friend their age, both plenty fond of cocks, after they had dated around with twenty-somethings.

I had relevant anecdotes of my own, some from a recent stint on the editorial board of *Salacious*, a sex magazine advertising queer, feminist, anti-racist "radically sex positive thought provoking superhot porn."[1] In the magazine, cocks figured prominently. Often, they underscored queer gender, particularly when detachable. Sometimes, texts ended with a character removing a cock that until then had seemed to have flesh-like workings. Also, similar to something I noted in nonfictional contexts, characters frequently used words such as *hard* and *wet* independent of body-generated stiffening or lubrication, which I took to designate queer gender, too. Since submissions overall reflected mainstream ageism and ableism about who is hot, they generally did not, for example, include characters invoking bodily responses previously at the ready. I wondered if times had changed on depicting arousal.

I had a bit of material evidence to support that claim, like the porn stories running across the bottom of one of my favorite texts ever: the 1994 book *Her Tongue on My Theory* by the performance collective Kiss and Tell. Despite much shape-shifting, gender play, and role play as the lesbian protagonist encounters the same character in different guises, cocks are scarce. The one telltale bulge, discerned when this mysterious character presents as male, turns out to be a "ruse," hiding an essential "Her."[2] Then again, I had a doll from the period that Jed Bell had made for me by transforming Barbie's boyfriend Ken into Passing Butch Glenn. The doll came with the sticker QUEER GIRLS MAKE ME HARD in a kind of transmasculine articulation common in *Salacious*.

I wanted to supplement my meager, contradictory, haphazardly culled evidence. So, in 2017, when my research assistant Grace Glasson was in her mid-twenties and I was in my late fifties, I sent her to the Brown University archives to study *On Our Backs* (OOB), a well-known sex magazine with the tagline "Entertainment for the Adventurous Lesbian" that ran from 1984 to 2006. I asked her to look at the years 1990–95, which corresponded, I thought, to the "back then" of many rumblings. I hoped less to flesh out a lost past, which the study of one source would hardly accomplish, than to find some juicy tidbits that would help me think about current nostalgias. In writing about the archival study of sexualities, Anjali Arondekar points out that loss is a structuring component of many approaches to the past, ranging from postcolonial to more mainstream studies of what has been mystified, marginalized, or stolen. Arondekar suggests that we "abandon the language of search and rescue and focus instead on sexuality as a site of radical abundance."[3] I wanted to flesh out some abundance.

I hadn't expected the lavender dildo to emerge as a historical marker, but Grace was definitely onto something. Lavender dildos figured prominently in early feminist dildo production and sales, born of collaboration between an inventor seeking assistive technologies for people understood to be missing something and early feminist sex toy purveyors intent on showing that they were lacking for nothing at all. Dell Williams, who started Eve's Garden in 1974, and Joani Blank, who opened Good Vibrations in 1977, didn't initially want to sell dildos. Who needed to insert something anyway, and why did it have to resemble a penis?[4] They wanted to promote clitoral orgasms, busting the myth that women primarily climaxed vaginally. At least, that was the dominant phrasing of the myth. More precisely, myth busting was predominantly imagined to benefit cisgender women, and it more precisely served people with the kind of vagina and clitoris traditionally identified as such. Just as people might understand arousal and getting hard or wet independent of the body mechanics generally associated with those terms, people may identify as a clit or penis something that doesn't ordinarily bear that label or they may feel the presence of bodily elements in other ways.

Eventually Williams and Blank responded to consumer demand. Williams collaborated with dildo designer Gosnell Duncan, a disability rights activist who had been trying to improve on available models after an accident left him with partial paralysis.[5] Many dildos he created for her were pink or lavender. Duncan also created the "silicon dildo by Scorpio in lavender, cream, or chocolate" featured on a 1991 *OOB* ad that boasts the intimate involvement of *OOB* staff: "Designed by *On Our Backs* based on office tests and consumer requests, this dildo's style and durability is the best ever (no veins!)."[6]

The lavender dildo thus had a feminist pedigree. The color also had general queer associations and could call up radical lesbian feminism more specifically, as in the term *lavender menace*. Appropriated from lesbian-hostile Betty Friedan for a 1970 action against lesbian exclusion from mainstream feminism, the term continued to circulate as shorthand for the radical potential of dykes and other queer people to disrupt heteropatriarchy.

Lavender as queer, sometimes menace-ing, circulates still. So do lavender dildos but without the same currency in queer and feminist contexts. Feminist sex shops rarely feature them. I contacted Toronto's Come as You Are Co-operative (CAYA), an "anti-capitalist and feminist" sex shop,[7] after a friend thought she remembered a sale that included one dildo in its lavender version only. She had remembered correctly. Worker-owner Jack Lamon told me that CAYA's customers don't want lavender dildos; the distributor had mistakenly shipped two unordered cases that the store put on sale to try to get rid of them.[8] Nomia, in Portland, Maine, doesn't carry them either. Same reason: They can't move the product.[9] The websites for Babeland and Good Vibrations, which let consumers search dildos by color, offer some models in deep purple but none in lavender. Meanwhile, the mass-market web retailer Dear Lady, which boasts "over 3 million sex toys sold," marketed at least into 2019 a lavender version of the Doc Johnson Mr. Softee Pastels Dong. But its ad copy suggested an imagined consumer less queer than delicate in body or sensibility: "Soft on the eyes and soft to the touch," this dildo is "sensually soft and pliable for easy insertion."[10]

What changed? How did lavender dildos, once sold primarily in feminist sex shops, relocate to the mainstream? The answer is partly, I think, that they always carried more fraught associations than my account of *OOB*'s enthusiastic endorsement might suggest. To begin with, lavender could have troublesome implications in terms of what might be called racial noncontent. A white friend remembered lavender dildos as nonracist, maybe because they enabled her to sidestep dominant offerings in what Susie Bright, a founding editor of *OOB*, called in 1989 a "world that 'Doc Johnson' had abandoned to mediocrity," filled with dildos colored in "D.O.A. Caucasian."[11] But avoiding an approximation of your skin tone might have different implications if your skin makes you a target rather than an agent of racism. In "What's Race Got to Do with It?," a 1991 editorial for the Black lesbian erotic magazine *Black Lace*, Alycee J. Lane recounts that a friend seeing her mauve dildo screamed "Eeek!! What *race* issues do you have???"[12]

Whether or not she had race issues, her purchase options certainly did. Lane tried to buy a brown dildo at a "well-known, respectable sex shop" to photograph for the magazine because, "What would women think, seeing this used mauve dildo strapped to brown thighs? Honey, *please*." The salesperson could direct her only to a box of two-foot-long *"monstrosities"* in a package labeled "Big Black Dick." The insertable size in brown, she was told, had quickly sold out as usual. Both what was missing and what was available—which did not include a Big White Dick—point to the fetishizing of Black cisgender men as outsized, hypersexual, exotic, and dangerous.

Discussing Lane's account of this incident, Kai M. Green writes, "Black lesbian sex toy shopping was not just about a sex act; it was also political, entangled with capitalism and labor. The black or brown dildo was not just a dildo; it could not be detached from the black body ideologically, the cisgender stereotyped mandingo figure."[13] Capitalism and labor also contribute to why Doc Johnson got into lavender dildos and Dear Lady sells them. Stocking large inventories, they can serve more diverse markets. Cheap labor, besides cheap materials, must also factor into the low prices—in 2017 I spent about $14 on a Mr. Softee, which still reeked from off-gassing three years later—though the higher cost of fancier dildos does not by any means guarantee well-paid workers in manufacture, sales, or shipping.[14]

Lavender also lost some of its earlier purpose among feminists to distinguish the dildo from flesh insertables. Heather Findlay recounts in a 1995 essay about the lesbian "dildo wars," carried on in *OOB* and *Black Lace* among many locations on the page and off, that lesbians at the time sometimes rejected dildo use altogether and not always only for themselves, arguing that feminist and/or lesbian women didn't or shouldn't want one.[15] Wanting one meant wanting maleness or masculinity, a penis on or in you, heteropatriarchal sex like where a man fucks and thereby dominates a woman. Jill Posener told me a striking anecdote about how intense hostility to dildos could be. With Bright, she coedited *Nothing but the Girl: The Blatant Lesbian Image, a Portfolio and Exploration of Lesbian Erotic Photography*.[16] When the book came out in 1996, well-known lesbian artist Tee Corinne emailed the editors an itemized list of images with dildos, protesting their prevalence. Despite being honored as a featured artist in the book, she considered lesbian desire ill-represented overall.[17]

Lurking here, I think, besides a justifiable refusal of heteropatriarchal presumptions about the penis as the be-all, end-all agent of power and pleasure, is the sexual dimorphism that Hilary Malatino identifies as a dominant conceptual framework with far-reaching limitations. Sexual dimorphism is the idea that all people have a true sex, male or female, making any mixedness a disorder, defect, or disability rather than, for instance, wondrous, desirable, or, even, real.[18] Consequences range from medical intervention forced on people deemed as yet insufficiently male or female to failures of varying import in imagination and understanding.

One hilarious example for me appears in a 2013 account by John S. Hall, front man for the band King Missile, about the genesis of their 1992 cult hit "Detachable Penis." He'd been inspired by a *Village Voice* article about a lesbian who "had the feeling that she could be male when she wanted to—you could just strap it on or take it off at will and you're a different gender." But once he started writing, that concept "didn't seem workable." So, he turned it into a song about a (seemingly cisgender) man who enjoys having a detachable penis. He rents it out and leaves it at home if he expects it to get him into trouble. But after losing it while drunk at a party, he is desperate to retrieve it. He feels "like less of a man" when it's gone for too long and hates sitting down to pee. Eventually, he finds it on a street vendor's blanket, laid out with other goodies like a broken toaster oven, and buys it back. That's all somehow more workable than a tale about gender shifting with attachables.

I don't want to make too much of a jocular interview among alternative-music guys about a song written many years earlier. But its logics resonate with the anti-dildo posture of some feminists and the history of the lavender dildo itself. There are men, and there are women. You are, and remain, one or the other. Men have a penis. It's there or missing, intact or disabled. Women don't have one. To approximate having one is to approximate maleness, or want to. That's bad. In this context, as Lamon well put it, lavender was often a "safe" choice as opposed to an exciting or beloved one. "If you wanted to have strap-on sex (which was pretty subversive at the time), but didn't want anyone to accuse you of re-enacting oppressive heterosex, your dick better be an appropriate non-realistic colour. As such, there were a lot of lavender cocks kicking around our feminist sex shop."[19]

Lavender, to put it another way, helped to present a silicone cock as a technology of pleasure rather than of gender. This goal is still visible on the website of Wet for Her, the one company I found that prominently features lavender (though labeled as purple) dildos. It emphasizes that their products are "not flesh-tone or intended to look realistic" and are conceived especially for lesbian couples.[20] That by "realistic" they mean penis-like stands out if you consider their "signature" invention, the finger extender. It looks enough like two fingers that the feminist sex shop As You Like It categorizes it under "realistic dildos."[21] While no single cause explains the demotion of the lavender dildo, one is surely the increased support among feminist sex-product purveyors for the idea that dildos may be technologies of gender, too, one of the "tools," as Spectrum Boutique puts it, "that can be used to express or experiment with gender. . . . Whether you're gender fluid, non-binary, transgender, queer, or cisgender."[22]

Then again, don't count out the lavender dildo or cement retrograde meanings to it. Like dildos and cocks, meanings, with more and less difficulty and dependent on resources, can be detached, tucked away, adorned, repurposed, and differently embodied. As I wrote in "Page 27 of *The Godfather*" about people just about my age remembering a sex scene from that novel, interpretations have trends and variations, historical specificity and personal idiosyncrasy. In fact, while I just described the song "Detachable Penis" as remarkably rooted in cisgender dimorphism given its topic, I first learned of it in the mid-1990s when I received it on a mixtape from someone who sent me a lot of songs, including Salt-N-Pepa's "Whatta Man," that he had gathered as ripe for trans interpretation, especially in a context far from replete with explicit trans material.

Besides, shades of purple continue to please. Lesbians sometimes buy them as the obvious choice.[23] Queer, trans, and genderqueer people enjoy them, too, and skin-like colors have hardly taken over. When I spoke with Lamon in summer 2018, he told me that the surprise hottest CAYA sellers for the past year and a half had been tie-dye and rainbow-striped dicks.[24] Back at *Salacious*, where my inquiry started, there's a hot touch of lavender. It's around the edges of that dildo on the home page going right into a happy mouth.[25]

Cis-Skeletal

 On the Day of the Dead 2014, while visiting the Mission San Xavier del Bac in Tucson, Arizona, I semi-accidentally witnessed the concluding ritual of the Fourteenth Annual Day of the Dead pilgrimage sponsored by the Coalición de Derechos Humanos (CDR) for people who over the previous year had died crossing the border from Mexico to the United States. Each was represented by a cross, marked either with the person's name or *desconocido, desconocida*, or *desconocido/a*.

In addition to reflecting the normative gendering of Spanish adjectives, the use of three gendered forms for *unknown* suggests several important, laudable intentions. These include resistance to sexist practices of using male gender indicators for unidentified people in general, as in such phrases as "man's inhumanity to man," and a desire to present the unknown dead with as much of an identity as possible. In some circumstances, o/a also designates people who identify themselves apart from binary gender, like the subsequent uses of @ and then *x*, as in *Chican@* or *Latinx*. Those forms have wide-ranging meanings and politics. Alan Pelaez Lopez writes, for example, "Transgender and gender-nonconforming Latin Americans living in the U.S. have used the 'X' as a reminder that their bodies are still experiencing a colonization invested in disciplining them to fit a standard gender identity, gender presentation, sexual orientation, and a particular sexual performance."[1] An enduring feature of coloniality, as María Lugones writes, comes from "the brutal imposition of the modern, colonial, gender system."[2] I think that here, however, o/a primarily invokes, and often indexes, the desecration of people found without enough physical or material evidence to classify them by gender. In so doing, it also magnifies the indictment of US border practices that since the mid-1990s have contributed to the rise in deaths in the Sonoran Desert.

Yet what remains *do* enable classification by gender? It struck me watching the ritual that I was not only watching a loving, political act of respect, witnessing, and resistance, of welcoming among the living the spirit of those who had died under brutal regimes of exclusion. I was also watching gender attribution unconfirmed by gender identity, a process that can easily result, must certainly sometimes result, in misgendering. Kody Hersh had a similar, more personal reaction on seeing gendered grave markers in Douglas, Arizona, of unidentified people who had died crossing the border: "I imagine my body laid to rest under a headstone that reads 'Unknown Woman,' at the end of a lifetime spent claiming the dignity and integrity of my male, genderqueer, and trans identities."[3] Those crosses and grave markers reflect processes of gendering that in other situations we often, rightly, regard as patently ignorant or hostile. I think, in particular, of situations in which a person, dead or living, who cannot refuse inspection for some reason, and there are many, becomes subject to claims that the inspector's classification system determines their gender regardless of how they have presented or classified themselves.

If that last sentence seems long-winded to you, it might be because I avoided the common phrases that make such narratives smooth going: phrases like "revealed to be [insert (mis) gender(ing) here]" or "born [insert given name here]." The latter, used in other contexts, too, such as indicating an alias or a surname before marriage, is so common as to obscure that it is always false. Babies do not emerge with names attached. More importantly, both phrases work to underplay the violence of misgendering and to naturalize some of its components. These include the presentation of takeover as discovery as it is used in narratives of colonization and conquest—I imagine that I have *found* your gender when really I have stolen the right to name it. They also include the rooting of gender truths in the body, the notion that x bones, genitals, chromosomes, and/or hormones add up to being y gender.

From this standpoint, nonconsensual gendering starts the life of everyone who is assigned a gender at birth that even people who know better persist in assigning them. Susan Stryker describes the violence wrought, not only on the child, in recounting her pain and "transgender rage" after participating in the birth of her lover's child, when someone in the room declared, "It's a girl," though everyone there knew full well that inspection does not always correctly predict gender. She writes: "A gendering violence is the founding condition of human subjectivity; having a gender is the tribal tattoo that makes one's personhood cognizable."[4] The understanding of gender as foundational contributes to the desire to provide unidentifiable remains with at least a gender and necessarily contributes to practices that occasion misgendering.

This piece considers the cis-skeletal presumptions involved in gendering the dead, using the specific example of people who die trying to cross the border south of Tucson. It's one of the longer pieces in the book because it requires, I think, a series of internal hip checks, raising issues and points that I juxtapose without smoothing transitions. They collide with, redirect, and undo each other. I don't want to smooth that over.

While the word *dehumanize*, like *objectify*, is thrown around often enough to lose meaning, for people trying to cross the border illegally south of Tucson dehumanization characterizes every stage, from the conditions that impel and attend migration to the consequences of being caught or killed—a term appropriate for dying in the desert given the blockage of nonlethal routes. More than two thousand people have died in the Sonoran Desert in the twenty-first century. Primary among the culprits is the US government's border strategy, developed in the early 1990s, of "prevention through deterrence," including Operation Blockade in the El Paso, Texas, region, begun in 1993; Operation Gatekeeper in San Diego, begun in 1994; and Operation Safeguard in Tucson, begun in 1995.[5] Closing off easier points of entry into the United States, the US government forced people to attempt more treacherous crossings. In the Tucson sector, which experienced 38 percent of the deaths during migration along the US-Mexico border between 1998 and 2012, the length of time and difficulty of path grew as border control increased. So, too, as the authors of "Structural Violence and Migrant Deaths in Southern Arizona" point out, did the number of people who died and the percentage of those who died by exposure, an extraordinarily painful death.[6]

Innumerable documents and policies reveal dimensions of the dehumanization involved. A 1998 US Department of Justice investigation of Operation Gatekeeper's early years frames undocumented border crossers as numbers to be picked off. This happens both through the use of such terms as *strategic advantage*, which suggests controlling people for sport, and in a section on the confusion, suspicion, and disgruntlement of border patrol agents when they could no longer demonstrate successful job performance by high numbers of apprehensions but, instead, had to document lower numbers.[7]

Today, success depends simultaneously on deterrence and higher numbers. Quotas built into the federal budget almost every year beginning in 2010 eventually required, in fiscal year 2020, more than $2.7 billion for fifty-four thousand available prison detention beds daily for undocumented border crossers.[8] Along with quota deals given to for-profit prison corporations, they govern the fact, conditions, and length of incarceration.

People caught crossing the border illegally may then face Operation Streamline, begun in 2005, which conducts criminal hearings for seventy to eighty people per session, brought before the judge eight at a time. When I attended a hearing on April 15, 2015, in Tucson, I timed the procedure for one particular group of eight. It took eleven minutes, even with Charles R. Pyle, reputed to be the "slow" judge,[9] presiding. Pyle's response to one person's plea for lenience in their brief opportunity to speak on their own behalf suggests how failure to differentiate among individuals charged with migrating illegally breeds more failure to differentiate, redoubling racial stereotypes. The person before the judge cited the four children who needed them. "I'm sure everyone in this room could tell the same story," Pyle replied. What presumptions and stereotypes make him so sure? Do they concern brown people, brown people migrating north, poor people? Does he imagine simple, uniform sexuality and gender identity, uniform family arrangement, undisciplined breeders?

People who die trying to cross the border may not be identified for various reasons. These include: insufficient person power to handle the huge number of cases, which speaks to values in distribution of resources; the limited evidence exacerbated by conditions of death in the Sonoran Desert; exclusions from databases that themselves maintain geopolitical borders; and the anti-paper trail involved in trying to cross a border without authorization.

Side step one: I've written so far as if the fact of monitoring national borders can go without saying. It never can, as the border involved here well illustrates. Reshaped in 1848 by the Treaty of Guadalupe Hidalgo, which ceded massive areas from Mexican to US rule, and again in 1853–54 by the Gadsden Purchase, or Treaty of La Mesilla, the border colloquially known as the US-Mexican border runs across Tohono O'odham land. This has numerous effects on Tohono O'odham people, who both encounter migrating people passing through and deal with the consequences of being mistaken for them by border patrol workers using brown skin as a sign for illegal. Border regulation technologies, like borders themselves, also have an important, laden history. For example, as Radhika Mongia emphasizes, the passport is of relatively recent origin compared to the forever that passports seem to have been around.[10]

All forms of documentation have history and politics, including others that might make people crossing the border identifiable in US databases. Consider the case of Dilcy Yohan, featured in the 2013 documentary *Who Is Dayani Cristal?*, by filmmaker Marc Silver, which follows the forensic, administrative, and nonprofit work involved in identifying the remains of people who die trying to cross the border south of Tucson. Yohan, found in 2010, was identified not by the large tattoo on his chest reading "Dayani Cristal," which the title implies might hold the key, but by rehydrated fingerprints that yielded a police record.[11] In 2006, during a previous stay in the United States, Yohan was arrested on what the film terms "minor drug charges" in a small town outside of Portland, Oregon, and deported instead of imprisoned there. Notice again the importance of racism and anti-immigrant hostility, which likely factored into Yohan's fate, given decades of disproportionate drug arrests for people of color and changing regulations that lowered the severity of convictions triggering deportation.[12]

To restate succinctly before I shift directions again, people crossing the border without legal documents do so within what Catriona Sandilands calls "a bio/necropolitical context multiply predicated on their absolute dehumanization."[13] In other words, governmental and other institutional policies and practices mark them, in effect, for early death: both overtly violent death and the harsh, wearing conditions of living that Lauren Berlant well analyzes as slow death.[14] That dehumanization reveals itself partly as a screaming failure to differentiate among people migrating or to see them as individuals with lives and connections that matter.

Side step two: I had never considered that the term *migrant* itself can be dehumanizing until I heard Melissa Autumn White suggest at a conference that referring to someone as a migrant made migration everything about them.[15] Tellingly, when I edited this section with that critique in mind, I could frequently simply replace *migrants* with *people*.

In this death-dealing context, provisional gender assignment serves an understandably revered purpose: to return people to their loved ones, offering an end to uncertainty and a chance to grieve. Beyond the realm of the individual, recording gender also works against the erasure of fundamentally gender-marked aspects of life and death, including gender-based violence, such as femicide.

Yet moving against this dis-individuation and dehumanization is fraught with trouble, beginning with a power in the right to look that you cannot separate yourself from by recognizing that such power exists. In "The Ambivalent Archive," Angela Garcia writes about the numerous ways in which power inheres in research, from viewing, categorizing, and ordering materials to engaging with people you study.[16] This really came home to me at the Operation Streamline hearing. Sometimes you figure out in the middle of fieldwork that maybe you shouldn't be doing what you are doing. Witnessing unjust plea deals handed out at the rate of fifty an hour, I learned a lot. I understood more deeply the absolute fraudulence of consent in those deals and learned details I wouldn't know otherwise, like the judge's presumptions that every person awaiting his judgment could tell the same family story.

Yet it also made vivid and visceral why *apprehend* means both capture and perceive. I couldn't position myself apart from the violence of watching. After each set of eight cases, the people sentenced filed out in shackles, just to the front and right of me. I could choose to look or look away. In contrast, they could not avoid being the object of my sight, though they might, as many did, avoid looking back. For a moment, I wished that I could fill my eyes with a legible message of solidarity, support, compassion, and good prison-abolition, border, and anti-detention politics. But why exactly would I want to project that, for whose view or benefit? As I sat there, I'm embarrassed to admit, I wanted to distinguish myself from the (other) nice older white lady in my row, who was witnessing as part of her faith-based activist practice before heading back north to do community education in rural Minnesota. We were both comfortably resourced white people watching people of color made spectacle partly because they lacked the resources that helped us into observer seats. We each occupied roles that, as the authors of *Decolonizing Ethnography* explain, retain elements of power imbalance grounded in their colonial roots, elements that persist across better intentions and research design.[17]

Those imbalances also contribute to and come from habits of thinking about whose lives and ties matter most. For example, *Who Is Dayani Cristal?* works against the kind of dis-individuation I discussed by sharing particulars in the life of one person. The film introduces us to Yohan's wife, children, father, and friends, brings us home with Yohan after he has been identified, and distinguishes him visually by having the famous actor Gael García Bernal, who coproduced the film, re-create Yohan's attempted journey from Honduras to Arizona.

Focusing on one person has many narrative and explanatory advantages. Yet the representation of Yohan—and the issues and people his portrayal represents—would benefit from actively indicating that his gender, family arrangements, and sexuality might be otherwise. We don't explicitly meet or hear about queer people or learn that shelters along the migration route, like the one Bernal-as-Yohan visits, sometimes shelter, or refuse to shelter, people who are trans, gender-nonconforming, or nonbinary, as Martha Balaguera details in her ethnographic work on the embodied experiences of *chicas trans* in transit across Mexico en route to the United States.[18] Considering the film's use of fictionalizing strategies, the limited cast of characters is even more notable.

It is not that I imagine another version of the film that would simply populate Yohan's context more diversely. Remember the assumptions of Judge Pyle that everyone in his courtroom could tell the same story, conforming to a racialized vision of normative gender and sexuality. I want to avoid making any such presumptions about Yohan, though the film invites us to do so. As far as interviews with people close to Yohan indicate, Yohan identifies as male, conforming to the gender and name first assigned to him, as opposed, for instance, to what Yohan's tattoo might suggest—Dayani Cristal turns out to be his daughter's name. Yohan's life may indeed be well represented, but it also may not. Interviews with loved ones offer no guarantee, given what they might not know or reveal. When I think about populating the film differently, I also want to avoid the racialized visions of normative cisness or transness. For example, "*chicas trans*," Balaguera explains, is a geopolitically, racially, and economically situated identity that refuses dominant ideals of white womanhood, which like all gendered ideals, identities, and expressions are also geopolitically, racially, and economically situated.[19]

As I consider whom the film shows and does not, I am also wary about locating correctives to normative presumptions in strategies of visibility. Despite common notions that visibility represents, advances, or is required for liberation, visibility is no simple good. Legibility often harms rather than assists trans and gender-nonconforming people seeking to cross borders, legally or illegally.[20] The representation of harm or violence has troublesome consequences, too. As micha cárdenas and Princess Harmony Rodriguez, among others, have written about reposting brutalities on social media, we may cause mental and emotional harm by participating in the onslaught of re-presentation, regardless of intention to demonstrate or enact solidarity.[21] Dora Silva Santana observes that the "deaths of trans and black people mobilize more action than our living, our *vivência*," suggesting that the focus on the dead, even in reverence and as a call to action, gets in the way of supporting life, healing, community, and resistance.[22]

Still, the silences matter and, in *Dayani Cristal*, build on those of the film's informants. Bruce Anderson, the forensic anthropologist featured in the film, asserts a reigning principle of studying skeletal remains in a 2013 *New York Times Op Doc* video called *Bodies on the Border,* also produced by Silver, on the same topic: "We try to look for clues from the skeleton as to who this person might be, and we make some pronouncements on the various bones of interest. And [we] come up with what we call a biological profile. Was it a man or a woman?"[23] As bioarchaeologist Pamela Geller notes, researchers generally assume that the first job with skeletal remains is to identify their sex, especially via pelvic indicators. Also largely untended, Cathy Gere explains, are the complications and non-givens of bones. For example, ideas about race and gender shape the assessment of bones, and researchers use evidence of apparent race to gender them. This is just one way that bones do not live firmly on the nature side of nature/culture divides despite what their durability as remains and their reputation for baseline truth help them suggest. "We can beat around the bushes" or "we can get down to the bone," as a source ill-suited to the somberness of this topic nonetheless well puts it.[24] Bones also change with living, with how you use your body.[25]

Regardless of any complications, however, bones and whole skeletons, like all other bits or wholes of bodies, do not yield gender. They yield, at most, the gender someone was likely assigned at birth. This is core to cis-skeletal privilege: traveling with purported gender markers that work as gender-identity markers. Where normative binarism guides gendering, they can speak for you.

It's on the Template

 In 2016 I noticed that registering to use the website for my upcoming fortieth high school reunion required me to pick "male" or "female" on a drop-down menu for gender. So I posted a question to the reunion's Facebook page, asking if organizers could change the website. Surely, I suggested, not all of our classmates would pick one or the other. Could the form accommodate a fill-in answer or eliminate the question entirely? Did organizers actually need the answer?[1]

I learned several things from the responses classmates posted. First, high school can still be brutal, long after it's over, if you don't fit or like traditional gender categories. Some classmates told me, often in nasty, sarcastic, and hurtful ways, that I was inventing problems that didn't exist or, as one person put it, inserting my fist high into my rectum. Note the anti-queer vibe in the common expression about having something up your ass, given stereotypes about anal penetration being a gay thing.

Second, I learned I had some great classmates, including someone running the website who agreed immediately to look into it and one person who had first posted that I was "overthinking things." We then went back and forth so much that, several days later, *she* was accused of having "taken this way too far." In between, she asked me a lot of questions, including how many people I knew who did not identify as male or female and how I would discern that information without intrusively violating their privacy. In concert with other people who chimed in, we both learned a lot. She made me glad I had hung in there, even if we didn't emerge exactly on the same page.

Third, I learned that organizers did not actively decide to include a gender question. It came on the template for high school reunion websites they had bought from ClassCreator.com.

I reflected a lot about putting this piece after "Cis-Skeletal." It may seem grotesquely inappropriate—a hip check that ought to be illegal—to throw you to my high school reunion website after an essay about gendering of the skeletal remains of people who died under murderous conditions generated by the US government. The displeasure of one early reader underscored for me that a hip check is a power move and that I have aims that sometimes conflict. I want words like *generosity* and *collaborative* to come up when you think of me, and I also want to push you around. In addition, besides great differences in gravity, the topics of these pieces differ significantly in that the website implicitly asks for gender *identity* (though only people who consider themselves male or female can record theirs), which is precisely what people trying to identify human remains can rarely access.

I kept the pieces in this order because their disparity highlights the wide range of contexts in which related problems in gendering operate. Like the bioarchaeologist Pamela Geller discusses, the makers of the reunions template presumed that gender is part of the most basic information that, obviously, you'd want to know about someone. Name, address, phone, birth date, gender: those belong on the first page of a form that requires no other demographic information. The only other drop-down menu, on page 2, has an extensive list of options to help you specify military service. We could also talk about that.

Like countless forms asking whether we are male or female, this one contributes, partly because there *are* countless forms, to naturalizing the idea that two one-word options can handle the gender question. There are also countless publicized statistics that presume binary gender. Editing this paragraph in May 2020, a somber example dominated my thinking: the Monday-through-Friday press conferences of the Maine Center for Disease Control and Prevention. Each begins by announcing how many people in Maine have newly passed away from COVID-19, identified by age range, county of residence, and male or female gender. If you're one of those people who have always checked "male" or "female" on a form without having to think about it, the invitation to do so again can make it easier to forget what you know. One friend commented that she had answered the question without thinking about it, although, like a number of others who responded to me, she knew exactly what I was talking about as soon as I brought it up.

I think that's also true of many people trying to gender human remains. They have within reach the tools to understand gendering otherwise. So, too, as I learned from the important research of Karma Chávez, for many people in the Coalición de Derechos Humanos (CDR), which organized the Day of the Dead pilgrimage I discussed in "Cis-Skeletal" where people carried crosses assigning gender to the unknown dead. As Chávez details, the CDR had worked extensively with a local LGBTQ group, Wingspan. Far from being concerned only with the overlapping category of LGBTQ people who migrate, the groups worked to "overtly link anti-migrant and anti-queer oppression and to demonstrate solidarity between two seemingly separate communities." In 2006, when the region faced five ballot measures that aimed to harm queer people or people who will or have migrated without papers permitting them to do so, the groups issued joint statements on what they called "campaigns of dehumanization."[2]

Once binary gender is on the template, its insufficiencies can be harder to notice, easier to forget, and formidable to change. This holds in contexts dire and routine, laden and light—or at least seemingly light. The intensity of response I encountered on my high school class's Facebook page shows how fraught this issue can be, seemingly disproportionate to the context. This is partly because gender identity, attribution, inspection, and regulation are always enmeshed in so much: personal desires and interpersonal relations; racialized understandings of nature and training; different relations to ability, privilege, resources, and deprivation; the making, remaking, or reinscription of boundaries naturalized by templates, maps, and other devices that solidify divisions. Men's pants. Hipless hip checks. Native or migrant. Curved or straight. Visibly queer. Like me or not. The body for ballet. Or hula. Or shaking it. Or breeding.

How we divide people into categories has politics and political consequences. Chávez, drawing on feminists of color such as María Lugones, Gloria Anzaldúa, and Chela Sandoval, argues that collective work, like that of CDR and Wingspan, depends on "differential belonging" and "coalitional subjectivities." That means refusing to define and separate ourselves into categories based on normative ideals—about who has respectability, about what and whose domestic ties deserve support, about who occupies or belongs at the center or margins.[3]

Michael Hames-García offers a wonderful account of coalitional subjectivities in his short essay "When I Think of Pulse, I Think of Shakti." Describing the development of his own identity through the connections he made as a young gay Chicano studying in London at a dance club for queer South Asians, he writes about how that history affected his response to the deaths of forty-nine people at the Pulse nightclub in Orlando in 2016. He saw it not just as a tragedy for Latinx queers, the predominant victims and people most demographically like him, but also for the Muslim Americans facing Islamophobia that the killer's identity would fuel. "The connection and permeability of Shakti," he writes, "lay far from the proclamations of difference and separation that undergird nationalism, patriotism, and nativism." They also lay far from understandings of "brown bodies [as] interchangeable" that enable state, institutional, and individual perpetrators of suspicion, violence, and bigotry to paint their targets with a broad brush. "Because of how I understand my brownness and queerness, because of how I understand my humanity, I must reject any dichotomy between 'us' and 'them.'"[4] Cross-category connections can forge empathy and coalition.

Conclusion
HIP-CHECKED

 I've presented this book as a series of hip checks. As you have seen, it is also the product of hip checks on me. The death of Prince, for example, stopped my writing and shifted it, shifting it again as I reconsidered my plan to mark his death as an interruption, perhaps through the device of a text box. In the process, I thought more broadly about how visual and textual practices might participate in sidelining issues, particularly race, that I intend to hold central.

Another hip check: my friend's suggestion that I needed to "find another (s)way" rather than proceed by habit from positive to negative. That was one of many responses to early drafts that significantly reoriented me once, then again, in terms of form, content, and the relationship between them. I immediately saw the issue with the repeated route from positive to negative, but what about the destination "to negative"? I got to thinking about that more after I heard Lisa Bunker propose six principles of "post-binary writing" at a bookstore event in 2019 for *Zenobia July*, her novel about a trans girl cyber detective at a new middle school, written for people that age and beyond. Besides refusing given ideas of normal—one effect being that the cis rather than the trans or nonbinary characters "flutter around the edges" of her novels—the principles include not creating characters who are absolute villains, avoiding snark, and practicing love. Practicing, she emphasized, as in working at it. The way Bunker linked up enemy formation with the dichotomous thinking of gender binarism sent me back through my manuscript with an eye to the goals I had summarized as generosity of spirit.

I have already pinpointed for you some switches around snark. Feedback also prompted me to look for unduly pounding criticism, which was often marked, I discovered, by repeated use of such verbs as *fail to*. That's a complicated call within a project that studies racism and gender policing, aiming to understand and invite reflection on subtle aspects. What is pounding versus analyzing the subtleties or identifying repetition, breadth, or persistence? Also, is pounding always unwarranted? No, but I began to see my decisions more within an overall calculation of tone, goals, and space.

For example, one of those text boxes I abandoned addressed the politics of citation through my discovery that an author I had quoted was a powerful white man at a prestigious academic, predominantly white institution who had been protected by other powerful white men, using corrupt procedures at their disposal, after credible evidence that he had harassed a woman professor under his authority. Right there is *white men* as an institution, including people and modes of operating, that, Sara Ahmed explains, dominant citational practices shore up.[1] I could use my decision to eliminate the source to make a number of points about complicities of institutional privilege, both his and mine. Desiring to bypass his book, I assigned the task of surveying its sources to a paid student research assistant funded by my own employer, Bates College, which also propels me past website paywalls and offers other research support that helps me practice my citational politics. But drawing out those points seemed to require at least four hundred words. So I decided to use that space instead to share the fruits of better citational politics and to direct you to Ahmed's work on the topic, in both her book and a post on her blog. Besides aiming to learn from and share the work of feminist, anti-racist, queer, and decolonial thinkers, I try to include some sources readers don't have to pay for.

The last big hip check I want to talk about I have referenced before: I was hip-checked by my own body. That sentence you just read represents one of the rare times that I switched a verb to the passive voice. I did it late into the editing process, when I finally noticed that changing hormone levels generated within my body could only *feel* externally delivered. "I hip-checked myself" or even "my body hip-checked me" did not work as well, I thought, to convey the perception of an external assaulter.

Fans of "writing as thinking" and "writing to learn," which deserve their growing pedagogical popularity, sometimes plant them on the side of illumination. It can also serve mystification, especially when you have a stake in not learning something. I had a big stake here. As I described in "Clocking the Natural," I loved the notion, despite knowing about the harm and fraudulence, that my body both expressed my queer femme gender and revealed it to me—broadening my hips in feminine-coded ways just as I was letting other hints surface. Then, I realized one day about three decades later that, because menopause had depleted my estrogen production, I had gained weight the way my butch girlfriend had done long ago, helping to make us recognizable to others and to ourselves, or at least to me, as femme and butch. For a while, I blocked myself from seeing it, even when my clothes no longer fit right. I remember scrutinizing myself in the mirror, in the months after the 2016 presidential election, thinking, Sure, I'm skating a lot. But why, with all that comfort eating, haven't I gained the "Trump 15"? I had, in front.

I thought, primarily, that I should get over myself. After all, cis-skeletal advantage and the entrenchments of white supremacy had shielded me from many racialized barriers to gender self-determination, making it a luxury and privilege to experience feeling degendered as a new personal tragedy late into my sixth decade. Alison Kafer also asks us in *Feminist, Queer, Crip* to grapple with the ableist components in narratives of bodily loss and nostalgia, presuming a better past and dwelling over what's gone.[2]

I could contextualize my reaction, too, within the sexism that lurks, as Kai Cheng Thom suggests, in many body-hating scripts attributed to other causes, like wrong body discourse. In "This Trans Woman Never Felt 'Born in the Wrong Body'—And Here's Why That's So Beautiful," Thom writes that maybe it had been easy to hate her "physical self" because all women are taught to hate our bodies: "Our bodies exist in constant conversation with the expectations, desires, demands of others. We are taught that our bodies are always failing us, because they are failing to live up to the shape that other people have told them to be."[3] And/or/because of what other people will desire. In 2017, the year I recognized my de-curving in the mirror, "(I'm in Love with the) Shape of You" was the most streamed song on Spotify, sharing radio time with the crossover hit "Body like a Back Road," where the singer knows "every curve" of his lover like "the back of [his] hand."[4] I could situate mourning the departure of my curvy hips within the queer erotics of butch/femme and understand my fondness for them as a queer femme take on feminine norms. But why I loved my body that way and how I had read my hips—like, I will venture, all the shapes we're in love with, backroads and all—are informed by the toxic brew of sexism, transmisogyny, and cis-skeletal privilege in which they emerged, formed with raced, classed, and ethnic notions of ideal and excess.

Besides, there are many other ways to think about your body than as the right or wrong container of your authentic self. "We're in this together, my body and me," Mary Ann Saunders wrote about her paths to gender-affirming surgery, adding that she and her body are not separate entities as the limited language she has available might suggest. Yes and/yes but, here is how fat redistribution felt to me: like my body was stealing my queer gender.

Saunders offered a different, or additional, perspective when I wrote to her about it—and here we are corresponding as the friends Mary Ann and Erica:

It's so interesting how our bodies shape our relationships with ourselves, isn't it? Whether that's in a way that is troubling, as I think your experience must have been, or loving, as mine has been. I had the interesting experience stepping into the OR and pausing for a microsecond—where my brain was going "are you sure?"—but it was my body that propelled me forward, saying "you want this." And, of course, my body was right. I hope you've been able to refind your queer gender in your body as it is now, or maybe a new sense of queer gender that goes with your changed body.[5]

The last sentence unraveled me, both because it opened up the deep loss I felt and because it made me think that, besides grieving, I could remake or reinterpret my relationship between my body and my gender. That I hadn't considered it shook me, too. I was ensconced in a life full of people working to make their bodies suit their gender—which, I know, in varying ways describes all of us. I was deep into a book project putting forth an embodied model and metaphor of rethinking. Yet here I had been hip-checked, by my hips no less, and instead of shifting, I froze.

I suggested in "Queer Indirections" that objects of contemplation aren't as fixed as the association of contemplation with stillness might suggest. They change shape as you consider them or when you're trying to execute a simple transfer from place to place, memory to text, one text to another. Similarly, I think, unsticking needs a portion of staying where you are. As Samaa Abdurraqib suggested to me when I recounted another, related battle between my politics and my emotions, unsticking benefits immensely from the ability to hold contradiction.[6]

As I wrote in the introduction, I thought a lot while working on this book about how to abet expansive life and liveness in the face and exposition of death-dealing forces. Sometimes the WAIT, but! here is the bad news needs to be knocked again toward Yes, AND!. For example, Prince overspilled the text box I was writing about his death, partly because his death implicates pervasive racism. WAIT, but!, no, Yes, AND! consider even this one small document of his hips in action: a video released by Prince's estate in 2018 on the second anniversary of his death. Circulating as "Nothing Compares 2 U (OFFICIAL VERSION)," it consists of his 1984 recording of the song with a compilation of rehearsal footage from the same year in the studio where he recorded it.[7] There he is in the most extravagant queerly gendered liveness. Every outfit a profusion of touchable bump-ups—shimmer against muscle, fur against clouds, flashes of color or sequins, and heels, heels, heels. And the way he moves: At one point, he drops into a split and back up, then casually puts his hand into his pockets like hey, that was nothing. It's also choreographed debonair, enhanced, and sexed up, by the deep-V opening of his shirt, which is tucked into the slightly ballooned-out pants that give his hips one of their various presented shapes. Then there are the multiple-revolution turns, on the ground or in the air. They alternately, sometimes simultaneously, bespeak and exceed the dance training he'd had by then.[8] It is both grounding for virtuoso performance and material for playful disregard. Got it, but nope, not how *I'm* going to move.

You can see, knowing the ending, how right then and in the long term his hips might have been killing him. Those trademark splits, the slightly off-kilter jump landings, the twisting descents toward the floor and up, sometimes with one leg out to the side. Once, he drops to his knees, legs spread diagonally out behind him. It's like the butterfly stance responsible for so much hip injury in hockey goalies. Yet to stop at the litany of death dealing delivers a bit of death dealing itself against this joyous production of hips and high heels. The hip check, at best, I think, orients toward that glorious dance floor.

Afterword

HIP-CHECK YOUR WRITING — AN EXERCISE

 By standard definition, external forces deliver hip checks. They happen to you. Maybe, as in the sports I take the metaphor from, they occur within an arena where you expect them and might have trained to handle them. Some people argue, for instance, that forbidding hip-checking in the sports labeled women's and girls' hockey not only reflects sexist paternalism. It also performs a disservice to the players by failing to teach skills for responding to hits. Even if you train for them, however, hip checks knock you off course, sometimes more than or differently from what you have come to expect. I've talked in the book about events internal and external to the project that jarred or shifted me, and this project, dramatically.

As I've tried to advocate by example, <u>writers can also hip-check readers</u>. You probably weren't expecting to move from a piece on gendering human remains to the drop-down menu for gender on a class reunion website. But being shifted that way, I hope, opened up some new directions of thinking, pushed but not totally dictated by me, about the politics of inscribing gender binaries.

I've come to believe through writing this book that you can also intentionally hip-check your own writing. I talked in the introduction about trying to make muscle memory of experimentation. Developing a practice of hip-checking has helped me with that ongoing project and not just regarding form. While I have often perceived dislodging myself from traditional forms as the key to unsticking myself, I came to question how I understood experimentation during a workshop led by artist and writer Renee Gladman on the second day of a 2018 symposium called the Soup Is On: Experiment in Critical Practice.[1] Reflecting on what participants had done the day before, Gladman asked us to think about why we all seemed to go for poetic language, textual fragmentation, and other deviations from normative prose syntax when we experimented with writing differently. That was one of many hip checks during those two days to my own presumptions about how to pursue and recognize experimentation.

Here's an exercise to train your hip check. While you can do it on your own, I recommend collaborating with others who want to hip-check their writing, maybe in a small group or in workshop settings, as I first tried it out in the workshop Object Disturbance and Hip Check during the Soup Is On. First, pick something regarding your writing that you're stuck on: *stuck on* in the sense of mired, snagged, or vexed; possibly *stuck on* in the old-fashioned sense of crushed out. Attachments can feed immobility among other effects. Some graduate students at the workshop described feeling like they were dating their dissertations. It became a helpful way for many of us to think about our relationships to our writing—more or less dysfunctional, monogamous or poly, requiring in every case just the right snacks.

Why would you want to hip-check your writing? Maybe you have conclusions no longer as settled as you thought they were, a story no longer in the can. Maybe you have a project originally guided by academic training or other habits of thought and writing that you now want to depart from. For me, this has often involved abandoning the training I received in art history, where I began my academic career and learned to proceed by using objects to explain contexts or contexts to explain objects.

Maybe there's something you like just fine yet nonetheless imagine shifting course on. Maybe you can't get anywhere from an example, concept, phrase, or even word that had seemed just perfect for a purpose it isn't really serving. Sometimes I think I might have finished this book a lot sooner if I hadn't been so sure that being *stuck* on and *stuck on* hips should be its primary framing device. Maybe you want to be brave/r somehow. Or something else. I've gestured above to ways that I've been stuck. You might well be stuck in others.

Spend ten minutes writing down how you want to hip-check your writing. If you have a group of three or four to work with— or a bigger group divided up at first—begin with this writing activity. Think about including what's holding you back. Pleasure, comfort, gatekeeping, well- or ill-founded fears. Talk about what you've written with your small group and then, if there is one, the bigger group. Be prepared to be hip-checked into or out of your plans. If your experience is anything like mine, that's where the bravery and the sweetness of possibility come in.

notes

Hip Check: An Introduction

Parts of this piece appeared in "Hips," keyword for *TSQ: Transgender Studies Quarterly* 1, nos. 1–2 (2014): 98–99.

1 Shakira, "Hips Don't Lie," on *Oral Fixation, Vol. 2* (Los Angeles: Epic, 2005).

2 Eric A. Stanley, "Introduction: Fugitive Flesh: Gender Self-determination, Queer Abolition, and Trans Resistance," in *Captive Genders: Trans Embodiment and the Prison Industrial Complex*, ed. Eric A. Stanley and Nat Smith (Oakland, CA: AK Press, 2011), 11.

3 Ali Greey, "Queer Inclusion Precludes (Black) Queer Disruption: Media Analysis of the Black Lives Matter Toronto Sit-in during Toronto Pride 2016," *Leisure Studies* 37, no. 6 (2018): 662–76, https://doi.org/10.1080/02614367.2018.1468475.

4 Deandre Miles, "Facing a Complacent Campus: A Lesson in Discomfort," *Emory Wheel*, September 6, 2017, http://emorywheel.com/facing-a-complacent-campus-a-lesson-in-discomfort.

5 "Free the #BlackPride4," *No Justice No Pride*, February 12, 2018, http://nojusticenopride.org/free-the-blackpride4.

6 Mark Paul Richard, *Not a Catholic Nation: The Ku Klux Klan Confronts New England in the 1920s* (Amherst: University of Massachusetts Press, 2015), 204–6.

7 See Toby Beauchamp, "Introduction: Suspicious Visibility," in *Going Stealth: Transgender Politics and U.S. Surveillance Practices* (Durham, NC: Duke University Press, 2019), 1–23; and Talia Mae Bettcher, "Evil Deceivers and Make-Believers: On Trans-

phobic Violence and the Politics of Illusion," *Hypatia* 22, no. 3 (2007): 43–65.

8 A. Finn Enke, "The Education of Little Cis: Cisgender and the Discipline of Opposing Bodies," in *Transfeminist Perspectives in and beyond Transgender and Gender Studies*, ed. A. Finn Enke (Philadelphia: Temple University Press, 2012), 69–70.

9 Jian Neo Chen, *Trans Exploits: Trans of Color Cultures and Technologies in Movement* (Durham, NC: Duke University Press, 2019), 16.

10 Che Gossett quoted in Christina Ferraz, "Queerstions: What Does Cisgender Mean?," *Philadelphia Magazine*, August 7, 2014, https://www.phillymag.com/g-philly/2014/07/08/queerstions -cisgender-mean.

11 Antoinette Bueno, "EXCLUSIVE: Sheila E. on Prince: 'He Was in Pain All the Time, but He Was a Performer,'" *ET Online*, April 22, 2016, http://www.etonline.com/news/187302_exclusive _sheila_e_says_prince_was_always_pain.

12 Lorraine Berry, "Prince Did Not Die from Pain Pills—He Died from Chronic Pain," *Raw Story*, May 6, 2016, http://www .rawstory.com/2016/05/prince-did-not-die-from-pain-pills-he -died-from-chronic-pain.

13 Jay Sibara, "Disability and Dissent in Ann Petry's *The Street*," *Literature and Medicine* 36, no. 1 (2018): 1–26, 2.

14 Terri Kapsalis, *Public Privates: Performing Gynecology from Both Ends of the Speculum* (Durham, NC: Duke University Press, 1997), 39–41.

15 Bettina Judd, *Patient* (New York: Black Lawrence Press, 2014), 8.

16 C. Riley Snorton, *Black on Both Sides: A Racial History of Trans Identity* (Minneapolis: University of Minnesota Press, 2017), 19 and chapter 1 throughout.

17 Sally Markowitz, "Pelvic Politics: Sexual Dimorphism and Racial Difference," *Signs* 26, no. 2 (2001): 389–414, especially 406–9.

18 Angeletta K. M. Gourdine, review of *Red Nails, Black Skates: Gender, Cash, and Pleasure on and off the Ice*, by Erica Rand, *Feminist Formations* 26, no. 1 (2014): 191–94, 194.

1 · *If Men Don't Have Hips*

1 Women's Flat Track Derby Association (WFTDA), definition of "Hips," in glossary of "The Rules of Flat Track Roller Derby," January 1, 2020, https://rules.wftda.com/90_glossary.html.

2 C. J. Pascoe, "Multiple Masculinities? Teenage Boys Talk about Jocks and Gender," *American Behavioral Scientist* 46, no. 10 (2003): 1423–38, 1427.

3 NBA, "Rule No. 12: Fouls and Penalties," in "2018–19 NBA Rule Book," accessed December 20, 2019, https://official.nba.com /rule-no-12-fouls-and-penalties.

4 WNBA, "Official Rules of the Women's National Basketball Association, 2019," 71, accessed December 20, 2019, https:// ak-static.cms.nba.com/wp-content/uploads/sites/27/2019/05 /2019-WNBA-Rule-Book-Final.pdf; NBA, "NBA Officials Media Guide 2019–20," 95, accessed December 20, 2019, https:// cdn.nba.net/nba-drupal-prod/2019-20-NBA-Officials-Guide .pdf.

5 Devendra Singh, B. J. Dixson, T. S. Jessop, B. Morgan, and A. F. Dixson, "Cross-cultural Consensus for Waist–Hip Ratio and Women's Attractiveness," *Evolution and Human Behavior* 31, no. 3 (2010): 176–81, https://doi.org/10.1016/j.evolhumbehav.2009 .09.001.

6 Jim Gable, "Jennifer Lopez: The Reel Me," music video (New York: Epic, 2003).

7 Priscilla Peña Ovalle, *Dance and the Hollywood Latina: Race, Sex, and Stardom* (New Brunswick, NJ: Rutgers University Press, 2010), 133.

2 · *Showing and Telling*

1 USFSA, "2020 Official Figure Skating Rule Book," July 2019, 175, https://www.usfigureskating.org/about/rules.

2 Debi Thomas, interview by Allison Manley, *The ManleyWoman SkateCast*, August 24, 2009, http://www.manleywoman.com /episode-30-debi-thomas.

3 Claudia Rankine and Beth Loffreda, "On Whiteness and the Racial Imaginary: Where Writers Go Wrong in Imagining the Lives of Others," *Literary Hub* (blog), April 9, 2015, https:// lithub.com/on-whiteness-and-the-racial-imaginary (adapted from the foreword to Rankine and Loffreda, eds.,*The Racial Imaginary: Writers on Race in the Life of the Mind* [New York: Fence Books, 2015]).

4 Ellyn Kestnbaum, *Culture on Ice: Figure Skating and Cultural Meaning* (Middletown, CT: Wesleyan University Press, 2003), 119, 141–42.

5   Talia Mae Bettcher, "Evil Deceivers and Make-Believers: On Transphobic Violence and the Politics of Illusion," *Hypatia* 22, no. 3 (2007): 43–65.

6   Kai M. Green, "Troubling the Waters: Mobilizing a Trans* Analytic," in *No Tea, No Shade: New Writings in Black Queer Studies*, ed. E. Patrick Johnson (Durham, NC: Duke University, 2017), 65–82, 71.

7   Brenna Munro, "Caster Semenya: Gods and Monsters," *Safundi: The Journal of South African and American Studies* 11, no. 4 (2010): 383–96; Katrina Karkazis and Rebecca M. Jordan-Young, "The Powers of Testosterone: Obscuring Race and Regional Bias in the Regulation of Women Athletes," *Feminist Formations* 30, no. 2 (2018): 1–39, 5. See also their book *Testosterone: An Unauthorized Biography* (Cambridge, MA: Harvard University Press, 2019).

8   Jaime Schultz, "Reading the Catsuit: Serena Williams and the Production of Blackness at the 2002 U.S. Open," *Journal of Sport and Social Issues* 29, no. 3 (2005): 338–57, 344.

9   Ryan Coogler, dir., *Black Panther* (Burbank, CA: Marvel Studios, 2019).

10 The essay announced in the *Teen Vogue* Daily Newsletter had a slightly different title. Amira Rasool, "The French Open's Catsuit Ban against Serena Williams Is Racist," *Teen Vogue*, August 29, 2018, https://www.teenvogue.com/story/serena -williams-catsuit-ban-french-open-racist.

11 Janelle Monáe, "Q.U.E.E.N.," on *The Electric Lady* (Atlanta: Wondaland, 2013).

12 Carly Ledbetter, "Serena Williams: 'Doctors Aren't Listening' So Black Women Are Dying," *Huffington Post*, March 8, 2018, https://www.huffpost.com/entry/serena-williams-black-women -health-care_n_5aa156fce4b002df2c61c6aa.

13 Lauren Alexis Fisher, "Serena Williams Wears Empowering French Open Outfit One Year after Her Catsuit Ban," *Harper's Bazaar*, May 28, 2019, https://www.harpersbazaar.com/fashion /designers/a27611577/serena-williams-off-white-outfit-us-open.

3 · *Deep into Drivel*

1   Burger King, "Proud Whopper Campaign," YouTube video, posted July 2, 2014, https://video.search.yahoo.com/search /video?fr=mcafee&p=burger+king+proud+whopper+campaign #id=52&vid=63d0e6f8a8239349f77178c93744fcc5&action=click.

2 Human Rights Campaign, "Corporate Equality Index 2014: Rating American Workplaces on Lesbian, Gay, Bisexual and Transgender Equality," 56, accessed May 2, 2020, https://assets2 .hrc.org/files/assets/resources/CEI_2014_final_draft_7.pdf.

3 Riese, "Burger King's 'Proud Whopper' Isn't Anything for Gays to Be Proud Of," *Autostraddle*, July 2, 2014, http://www .autostraddle.com/burger-kings-proud-whopper-isnt-anything -for-gays-to-be-proud-of-243864.

4 RedazioneBrandNews, "BURGER KING—PROUD WHOPPER Case Study Film," YouTube video, posted June 23, 2015, https:// www.youtube.com/watch?v=2yohicMc4vU.

5 Matt Saccaro, "Unwrapping Burger King's Whopper of a Gay Marketing Ploy," *Daily Dot*, July 10, 2014, https://www.dailydot .com/via/burger-king-proud-whopper-marketing-ploy; Riese, "Burger King's 'Proud Whopper.'"

6 Natalie E. Norfus, Burger King® Diversity and Inclusion, Burger King website, accessed May 2, 2020, https://www .bk.com/diversity.

7 Lauren Michele Jackson, "We Need to Talk about Digital Blackface in Reaction GIFs," *Teen Vogue*, August 2, 2017, http://www .teenvogue.com/story/digital-blackface-reaction-gifs.

8 "Free the #BlackPride4," *No Justice No Pride*, February 12, 2018, http://nojusticenopride.org/free-the-blackpride4.

9 Meeting attended July 10, 2018, in Portland, Maine.

10 Mel Y. Chen, *Animacies: Biopolitics, Racial Mattering, and Queer Affect* (Durham, NC: Duke University Press, 2012), especially chapter 1.

4 · *TV Evidence*

1 Eric Plemons, *The Look of a Woman: Facial Feminization Surgery and the Aims of Trans-Medicine* (Durham, NC: Duke University Press, 2017), 13.

2 See Chase Strangio, "What Is a 'Male Body'?," *Slate*, July 19, 2016, https://slate.com/human-interest/2016/07/theres-no-such -thing-as-a-male-body.html.

3 Julia Serano, *Whipping Girl: A Transsexual Woman on Sexism and the Scapegoating of Femininity* (Emeryville, CA: Seal Press, 2007).

4 Erica Rand, "Court and Sparkle: Kye Allums, Johnny Weir, and Raced Problems in Gender Authenticity," *GLQ* 19, no. 4 (2013): 435–63, 442.

5 Katy Steinmetz, "The Transgender Tipping Point: America's Next Civil Rights Frontier," *Time*, May 29, 2014, http://time.com/135480/transgender-tipping-point.

6 Procter and Gamble, Tide advertisement, debuted on Fox, February 5, 2017; Tate Donovan, dir., "Too Fast, Too Furious," season 3, episode 4, *The Fosters* (Los Angeles: Freeform, August 1, 2017).

7 For early assessments of responses to gay window advertising see Wan-Hsiu Sunny Tsai, "Gay Advertising as Negotiations: Representations of Homosexual, Bisexual and Transgender People in Mainstream Commercials," in *Gender and Consumer Behavior*, vol. 7, ed. Linda Scott and Craig Thompson (Madison, WI: Association for Consumer Research, 2004), 1–26; Katherine Sender, "Selling Sexual Subjectivities: Audiences Respond to Gay Window Advertising," *Critical Studies in Mass Communication* 16, no. 2 (1999): 172–96.

8 Jill Soloway, executive producer, *Transparent* (Los Angeles: Amazon Studios, 2014–19).

9 On what's missing from the rosy account in the article see Reina Gossett, Eric A. Stanley, and Johanna Burton, *Trap Door: Trans Cultural Production and the Politics of Visibility* (Cambridge, MA: MIT Press, 2017); and Aren Aizura, ed., "Unrecognizable: On Trans Recognition in 2017," special section, *South Atlantic Quarterly* 116, no. 3 (2017): 606–46.

10 Email to author, August 14, 2019; [*sic*] is in original. See also Jen Richards, "Matt Bomer Playing a Trans Woman Is More Than Problematic—It's Dangerous," *NewNowNext*, June 16, 2017, http://www.newnownext.com/matt-bomer-anything-transgender/06/2017.

11 Alexandra Billings, "Jeffrey Tambor and Me," *Huffpost Personal*, May 10, 2018, https://www.huffingtonpost.com/entry/jeffrey-tambor-sexual-harassment-alexandra-billings_us_5af474bee4b0859d11d14647; Nico Lang, "Jeffrey Tambor Would Have Been Fired from 'Arrested Development' if His Accusers Weren't Trans Women," *Into*, May 15, 2018, https://intomore.com/culture/Jeffrey-Tambor-Would-Have-Been-Fired-From-Arrested-Development-If-His-Accusers-Werent-Trans-Women/aba43e3bb20841e8.

12 Lara O'Reilly, "The 5 Best Ads of Super Bowl 51," *Business Insider*, February 5, 2017, http://www.businessinsider.com/the-5-best-ads-of-super-bowl-li-2017-2/#2-tide-terrys-stain-4; Juddann Pol-

lack, "Tide Pulls Off a Super Bowl Surprise with Terry Bradshaw," *AdAge*, February 5, 2017, http://creativity-online.com
/work/tide-bradshaw-stain/50827.

13 Nathan Skid, "Anatomy of an Ad: Tide's Super Bowl Stain,"
AdAge, February 5, 2017, https://adage.com/article/video
/anatomy-ad-stain/307860.

14 Advertisement for Stouffer's lasagna seen on the October 31,
2017, episode of *The Young and the Restless,* airing on CBS.

15 Donovan, "Too Fast, Too Furious."

16 Megan Vick, "*The Fosters* Made TV History with Callie and
Aaron," *TV Guide*, August 22, 2017, http://www.tvguide.com
/news/the-fosters-elliot-fletcher-aaron-callie-sex-interview.

5 · *A Lothario in Gendered Jeans*

1 "Women of the Ivy League," *Playboy*, September 1979; Josh
Robertson, "The 10 Most Controversial *Playboy* Covers of All
Time," *Complex Pop Culture*, August 9, 2012, http://www
.complex.com/pop-culture/2012/08/the-10-most-controversial
-playboy-covers.

2 Joanna Russ, *Magic Mommas, Trembling Sisters, Puritans and Perverts: Feminist Essays* (Trumansburg, NY: Crossing Press), 1985.

3 Russ, *Magic Mommas*, 31.

4 Marilyn Hacker, letter to Joanna Russ, January 24, 1978, Joanna
Russ Papers, 1907–2014, coll. 261, Special Collections and University Archives, University of Oregon Libraries, Eugene.

5 Russ, *Magic Mommas*, 37.

6 Radclyffe Hall, *The Well of Loneliness* (1928; New York: Pocket
Books, 1956), 13.

7 Joanna Russ, draft of letter to editors who might assign reviewers
to *Magic Mommas, Trembling Sisters, Puritans and Perverts*, July 30,
1985. Copy. Joanna Russ Papers, coll., 261, Special Collections and
University Archives, University of Oregon Libraries, Eugene.

6 · *Hide and Seek*

Parts of this piece appeared in "Five Outings in Queer Indirection and the Ingredients of my Undoing," *Liminalities* 12, no. 2
(2016): 1–10.

1 *People* staff, "Call It the 'Dorothy Hamill,' the 'Wedge' or 'Wash
'n' Wear Hair,' It's the Coming Summer Look on Top," *People*,

April 26, 1976, http://www.people.com/people/archive/article
/0,,20066410,00.html.

2 Jo Ann Schneider Farris, "Skater Dorothy Hamill's Famous
   Wedge Haircut," LiveAbout.com, March 23, 2013, http://
   figureskating.about.com/b/2013/03/23/remembering-dorothy
   -hamills-famous-wedge-haircut.htm.

3 Suzy Kalter, "Samurai Stylist Suga Got a Wedge in with Dorothy, and Now He Clips Candy, Faye and Marie," *People,* August
   18, 1980, http://www.people.com/people/archive/article
   /0,,20077212,00.html.

7 · *Consensual Gender*

1 Leslie Feinberg, *Stone Butch Blues* (Ithaca, NY: Firebrand Books,
   1993); the author's twentieth-anniversary edition is available at
   lesliefeinberg.net, 28, 26.

2 Jewelle Gomez, "Layaway," in *It's So You: 35 Women Write about
   Personal Expression through Fashion and Style,* ed. Michelle Tea
   (Boston: Seal Press, 2007), 159–68, 167.

3 Jinthana Haritaworn, *The Biopolitics of Mixing: Thai Multiraciali-
   ties and Haunted Ascendancies* (London: Routledge, 2012), 20.

8 · *Clocking the Natural*

Parts of this piece appeared previously in "Hip Openers: On the
Visuals of Gendering Athleticism," in *Queer Difficulty in Art and
Poetry: Re-thinking the Sexed Body in Verse and Visual Culture,* ed-
ited by Jongwoo Jeremy Kim and Christopher Reed (New York:
Routledge, 2017), 154–67.

1 I make partial use here of fieldwork on figure skating, which I
   approached systematically as participant-observation research
   in the period from 2006 to 2012. I offer an extended discussion
   of methods in *Red Nails, Black Skates: Gender, Cash, and Pleasure on
   and off the Ice* (Durham, NC: Duke University Press, 2012), 6–8,
   20–25.

2 Conversation with Megan M. Burke, August 5, 2015.

3 Mary L. Gray, *Out in the Country: Youth, Media, and Queer Visibility in Rural America* (New York: New York University Press,
   2009), 19; Ernesto Javier Martínez, *On Making Sense: Queer Race
   Narratives of Intelligibility* (Stanford, CA: Stanford University
   Press, 2013), 5–6.

4 Carlos Ulises Decena, *Tacit Subjects: Belonging and Same-Sex Desire among Dominican Immigrant Men* (Durham, NC: Duke University Press, 2011), 17–18.

5 Eli Clare, *Exile and Pride: Disability, Queerness, and Liberation* (Cambridge, MA: South End Press, 1999), 112. See also Edward Ndopu and Darnell Moore, "On Ableism within Queer Spaces, or, Queering the 'Normal,'" *Pretty Queer*, December 7, 2012, https://sunylgbtq.wordpress.com/2015/07/17/on-ableism-within -queer-spaces-or-queering-the-normal.

6 Eli Clare, *Brilliant Imperfection: Grappling with Cure* (Durham, NC: Duke University Press, 2017), 14–15.

7 Mireille Miller-Young, *A Taste for Brown Sugar: Black Women in Pornography* (Durham, NC: Duke University Press, 2014), 4–9.

8 Momiala Kamahele, "'Īlio'ulaokalani: Defending Native Hawaiian Culture," in *Asian Settler Colonialism: From Local Governance to the Habits of Everyday Life in Hawai'i*, ed. Candace Fujikane and Jonathan Y. Okamura (Honolulu: University of Hawai'i Press, 2008), 76–98, 77.

9 Jodi Kim, "'There're a Billion Bellies Out There': Commodity Fetishism, the Uber-Oriental, and the Geopolitics of Desire in David Henry Hwang's *M. Butterfly*," in *Culture, Identity, Commodity: Diasporic Chinese Literatures in English*, ed. Tseen Khoo and Kam Louie (Montreal: McGill-Queen's University Press, 2005), 59–78, 65.

10 MyFootage.com, "1950s European Hula Hoop Craze," YouTube video, posted October 10, 2011, https://www.youtube.com /watch?v=-zovbmm8lX8.

11 "Hula Hoop Songs of 1958–59," *Music Weird* (blog), October 17, 2014, http://musicweird.blogspot.com/2014/10/hula-hoop -songs-of-1958-59.html.

12 Ryka Aoki, *He Mele a Hilo: A Hilo Song* (New York: Topside Signature, 2014), 6.

9 · *Gifts and Givens*

Parts of this piece appeared previously in "Hip Openers: On the Visuals of Gendering Athleticism," in *Queer Difficulty in Art and Poetry: Re-thinking the Sexed Body in Verse and Visual Culture*, edited by Jongwoo Jeremy Kim and Christopher Reed (New York: Routledge, 2017), 154–67.

1 Email conversation (anonymity requested), March 9, 2017.

2 Sara Ahmed, "Hello Feminist Killjoys," *feministkilljoys* (blog), August 26, 2013, (updated c. 2016), accessed December 20, 2019, https://feministkilljoys.com/2013/08/26/hello-feminist-killjoys.

3 Misty Copeland, with Charisse Jones, *Life in Motion: An Unlikely Ballerina* (New York: Touchstone, 2014), 21, 23, 48–52. On the writing relationship between Copeland and Jones, based partly on Copeland's extensive journaling since age fifteen, see Moira MacDonald, "Misty Copeland Talks about Food, Shyness and Her 'Ballerina Body,'" *Seattle Times*, March 16, 2017, https://www.seattletimes.com/entertainment/books/misty-copeland-talks-about-food-shyness-and-her-ballerina-body/.

4 Copeland, *Life in Motion*, 44, 42.

5 Copeland, *Life in Motion*, 188, 192, 165.

6 Copeland, *Life in Motion*, 206.

7 Copeland, *Life in Motion*, 168.

8 Copeland, *Life in Motion*, 265.

9 Copeland, *Life in Motion*, 74.

10 Copeland, *Life in Motion*, 207.

11 Copeland, *Life in Motion*, 21–26, 179–81.

10 · *Page 27 of* The Godfather

1 Mario Puzo, *The Godfather* (Greenwich, CT: Fawcett, 1969), 27–28.

2 Susie Bright, *Big Sex Little Death* (Boston: Seal Press, 2011), 64.

3 Puzo, *The Godfather*, 27.

4 Bright, *Big Sex*, 64.

5 Bright, *Big Sex*, 64; emphasis in original.

6 Sam Roberts, "Mary Fiumara, Mother in Indelible Prince Spaghetti Ad, Dies at 88," *New York Times*, February 4, 2016, https://www.nytimes.com/2016/02/05/business/media/mary-fiumara-mother-in-indelible-prince-spaghetti-ad-dies-at-88.html?_r=1.

7 Stephen Silver, "'The Godfather' Novel's Strange Vagina Subplot, Revisited," technologytell.com, October 8, 2014 (no longer available).

8 Puzo, *The Godfather*, 314–15.

11 · *Queer Indirections*

Parts of this piece appeared in "Five Outings in Queer Indirection and the Ingredients of my Undoing," *Liminalities* 12, no. 2 (2016): 1–10.

1 Michael Lehmann, dir., *Heathers* (Atlanta: New World Pictures, 1988).

2 Erica Rand, "Five Outings in Queer Indirection and the Ingredients of My Undoing," *Liminalities* 12, no. 2 (2016): 1–10.

3 Laurence O'Keefe and Kevin Murphy, "My Dead Gay Son," on *Heathers: The Musical (World Premiere Cast Recording)* (New York: Yellow Sound Label, 2014).

4 Miriam J. Abelson, *Men in Place: Trans Masculinity, Race, and Sexuality in America* (Minneapolis: University of Minnesota Press, 2019), 60–61.

5 Ryka Aoki, "When Something Is Not Right," in *Transfeminist Perspectives in and beyond Transgender and Gender Studies*, ed. A. Finn Enke (Philadelphia: Temple University Press, 2012), 195–202, 195.

6 Aoki, "When Something Is Not Right," 198.

7 Aoki, "When Something Is Not Right," 196.

12 · *Clocking the Unnatural*

Parts of this piece appeared in "The Proverbial Lavender Dildo" in *Queer Objects*, edited by Chris Brickell and Judith Collard (Dunedin, NZ: Otago University Press, 2019), 132–39.

1 *Salacious Magazine*, accessed May 6, 2018, http://salacious magazine.com.

2 Kiss and Tell, *Her Tongue on My Theory: Images, Essays, and Fantasies* (Vancouver: Press Gang Publishing, 1994), 90–91.

3 Anjali Arondekar, "In the Absence of Reliable Ghosts: Sexuality, Historiography, South Asia," *differences* 25, no. 3 (2014): 98–122, 98–99.

4 Lynn Comella, *Vibrator Nation: How Feminist Sex-Toy Stores Changed the Business of Pleasure* (Durham, NC: Duke University Press, 2017), 36–37, 54–56; Hallie Lieberman, *Buzz: The Stimulating History of the Sex Toy* (New York: Pegasus, 2017), 234.

5 Hallie Lieberman, "If You Mold It, They Will Come: How Gosnell Duncan's Devices Changed the Feminist Sex-Toy Game Forever," *Bitch*, no. 67 (Summer 2015), https://www.bitchmedia

.org/article/if-you-mold-it-they-will-come-dildo-history-feminist
-sex-toy-stores.

6 "Celebrate Sex!" ad in *On Our Backs*, November/December 1991,
49.

7 Come as You Are Co-operative (1997–2018) website, accessed
May 6, 2018, http://www.comeasyouare.com.

8 Jack Lamon, email to author, April 25, 2017.

9 Nomia Boutique, in-store conversation with employee, March
30, 2018.

10 Doc Johnson Mr. Softee Pastels Dong, 8″, DearLady.com, accessed May 6, 2018, http://www.dearlady.us/Doc-Johnson-Mr
-Softee-Pastels-Dong-Lavender/p/0255012N/?vp=3.

11 Susie Bright, "Great Balls from China and Other Tall Toys," *On
Our Backs*, March/April 1989, 6–7, 6.

12 Alycee J. Lane, "What's Race Got to Do with It?," *Black Lace*,
summer 1991, 21.

13 Kai M. Green, "Troubling the Waters: Mobilizing a Trans* Analytic," in *No Tea, No Shade: New Writings in Black Queer Studies*, ed.
E. Patrick Johnson (Durham, NC: Duke University Press, 2016),
65–82, 72–73.

14 Doc Johnson Mr. Softee Pastels Dong, 8″. It is also worth noting
that Bright sold on commission for Good Vibrations, so selling
dildos helped her make a living and, she argued, created a rift
with Blank that eventually caused Bright to quit. See Lieberman, *Buzz*, 237.

15 Heather Findlay, "Freud's 'Fetishism' and the Lesbian Dildo De-
bates," in *Out in Culture: Gay, Lesbian, and Queer Essays on Popular
Culture*, ed. Corey K. Creekmur and Alexander Doty (Durham,
NC: Duke University Press, 1995), 328–42, 328.

16 Susie Bright and Jill Posener, eds., *Nothing but the Girl: The Blatant Lesbian Image, a Portfolio and Exploration of Lesbian Erotic Photography* (New York: Freedom Editions, 1996).

17 Jill Posener, telephone conversation with author, March 30,
2018.

18 Hilary Malatino, *Queer Embodiment: Monstrosity, Medical Violence,
and Intersex Experience* (Lincoln: University of Nebraska Press,
2019), 53.

19 Jack Lamon email.

20 Wet for Her website, "About Us" page, accessed April 17, 2020,
https://www.wetforher.com/content/4-about-us.

21 As You Like It website, "Realistic Dildos" page, accessed April 17, 2020, https://asyoulikeitshop.com/product-category/dildos/realistic-dildos.

22 Spectrum Boutique website, "Gender" page, accessed April 17, 2020, https://spectrumboutique.com/shop/gender.

23 Samantha Irby, *We Are Never Meeting in Real Life* (New York: Vintage, 2017), 138.

24 Jack Lamon, telephone conversation with author, July 5, 2018.

25 *Salacious*. One of five rotating images on the home page, accessed May 6, 2018, http://salaciousmagazine.com/?ao_confirm.

13 · *Cis-Skeletal*

1 Alan Pelaez Lopez, "The X in Latinx Is a Wound Not a Trend," *EFNIKS*, September 13, 2018, accessed September 17, 2019, http://efniks.com/the-deep-dive-pages/2018/9/11/the-x-in-latinx-is-a-wound-not-a-trend (no longer available). Available on *Color Bloq*, accessed May 10, 2020, https://www.colorbloq.org/the-x-in-latinx-is-a-wound-not-a-trend.

2 María Lugones, "Toward a Decolonial Feminism," *Hypatia* 25, no. 4 (2010): 742–59, 743.

3 Kody Hersh, "Unidentified, but Known to God; Reflections of a Transgender CPT [Christian Peacemaker Team] Delegate," *CPTnet* (blog), March 5, 2015, http://www.cpt.org/cptnet/2015/03/05/borderlands-unidentified-known-god-reflections-transgender-cpt-delegate.

4 Susan Stryker, "My Words to Victor Frankenstein above the Village of Chamounix: Performing Transgender Rage," *GLQ* 1, no. 3 (1994): 237–54, 250.

5 Daniel E. Martínez, Robin C. Reineke, Raquel Rubio-Goldsmith, and Bruce O. Parks, "Structural Violence and Migrant Deaths in Southern Arizona: Data from the Pima County Office of the Medical Examiner, 1990–2013," *Journal on Migration and Human Security* 2, no 4. (2014): 257–86, 259, 262.

6 Martínez et al., "Structural Violence," 263, 270.

7 US Department of Justice, Office of the Inspector General, "Operation Gatekeeper: An Investigation into Allegations of Fraud and Misconduct (July, 1998)," subsection "Operation Gatekeeper," accessed December 20, 2019, https://fas.org/irp/agency/doj/oig/gatekpr/gktoc.htm

8 Department of Homeland Security, "FY 2020: Budget in Brief,"
   3, accessed December 20, 2019, https://www.dhs.gov/sites
   /default/files/publications/19_0318_MGMT_FY-2020-Budget
   -In-Brief.pdf.

9 Fernanda Santos, "Detainees Sentenced in Seconds in 'Streamline' Justice on Border," *New York Times*, February 11, 2014,
   http://www.nytimes.com/2014/02/12/us/split-second-justice-as
   -us-cracks-down-on-border-crossers.html?_r=1.

10 Radhika Viyas Mongia, "Race, Nationality, Mobility: A History
   of the Passport," *Public Culture* 11, no. 3 (1999): 527–56.

11 Marc Silver, dir., and Gael García Bernal, coprod., *Who Is Dayani
   Cristal?* (London: Pulse Films, 2014).

12 Even after decriminalization, arrests of minors for drug offenses
   particularly target people of color. Ashley Duchemin, "The Fra-
   gility of Legalization: Who's Cashing In on Marijuana?," *Bitch
   Media*, October 26, 2017, https://www.bitchmedia.org/article
   /marijuana-legalization/what-we-gain-expense-people-color.

13 Catriona Sandilands, unpublished response paper on the panel
   Unsettling Acts: Queering Ecotheory through Migration and
   Transience, American Studies Association Annual Conference,
   Toronto, October 8–11, 2015.

14 Lauren Berlant, "Slow Death (Obesity, Sovereignty, Lateral
   Agency)," chap. 3 in *Cruel Optimism* (Durham, NC: Duke University Press, 2011), 95–119.

15 Melissa Autumn White, unpublished roundtable statement in
   Trafficking Theory, Migrating Method, and Cross-Disciplinary
   Pedagogy: Sex Trafficking and Queer Migration Scholars in
   Conversation, American Studies Association Annual Confer-
   ence, Chicago, November 9–12, 2017.

16 Angela Garcia, "The Ambivalent Archive," in *Crumpled Paper
   Boat: Experiments in Ethnographic Writing*, ed. Anand Pandian and
   Stuart McLean (Durham, NC: Duke University Press, 2017),
   29–44.

17 Carolina Alonso Bejarano, Lucia López Juárez, Mirian A. Mi-
   jangos García, and Daniel M. Goldstein, *Decolonizing Ethnography: Undocumented Immigrants and New Directions in Social Science*
   (Durham, NC: Duke University Press, 2019), 28–29.

18 Martha Balaguera, "Trans-migrations: Agency and Confine-
   ment at the Limits of Sovereignty," *Signs* 43, no. 3 (2018):
   641–64.

19 Balaguera, "Trans-migrations," 641. For an important discussion of this matter in relation to the term, politics, and identity of *travesti* see Cole Rizki, "Latin/x American Trans Studies: Toward a *Travesti*-Trans Analytic," *TSQ: Transgender Studies Quarterly* 6, no. 2 (2019): 145–55.

20 Aren Z. Aizura, "Transnational Transgender Rights and Immigration Law," in *Transfeminist Perspectives in and beyond Transgender and Gender Studies*, ed. A. Finn Enke (Philadelphia: Temple University Press, 2012), 133–51, 137. See also Aren Aizura, "Introduction," *South Atlantic Quarterly* 116, no. 3 (2017): 606–11.

21 micha cárdenas, "Dark Shimmers: The Rhythm of Necropolitical Affect in Digital Media," in *Trap Door: Trans Cultural Production and the Politics of Visibility*, ed. Reina Gossett, Eric A. Stanley, and Johanna Burton (Cambridge, MA: MIT Press, 2017), 161–81, 171; Princess Harmony Rodriguez, "Caitlyn Jenner, Social Media and Violent 'Solidarity': Why Calling Out Abusive Material by Sharing It Is Harmful," *BGD* (blog), June 8, 2015, http://www.bgdblog.org/2015/06/caitlyn-jenner-social-media-and-violent-solidarity-calling-out-abusive-material-sharing-it.

22 Dora Silva Santana, "*Mais Viva!* Reassembling Transness, Blackness, and Feminism," *TSQ: Transgender Studies Quarterly* 6, no. 2 (2019): 210–22, 215.

23 Marc Silver, "Bodies on the Border," *New York Times*, August 17, 2013, https://www.nytimes.com/video/opinion/100000002390527/bodies-on-the-border.html, accessed May 10, 2020.

24 Eagles, "Heartache Tonight," on *The Long Run* (Los Angeles: Asylum, 1979).

25 Cathy Gere, "Bones That Matter: Sex Determination in Paleodemography, 1948–1995," *Studies in History and Philosophy of Biological and Biomedical Sciences* 30, no. 4 (1999): 455–71.

14 · *It's on the Template*

1 Post to the ETHS 76ers group page, July 3, 2016, thread July 3–7, 2016.

2 Karma R. Chávez, "Border (In)Securities: Normative and Differential Belonging in LGBTQ and Immigrant Rights Discourse," *Communication and Critical/Cultural Studies* 7, no. 2 (2010): 136–59, 146–47.

3 Chávez, "Border (In)Securities," especially 144–50.

4 Michael Hames-García, "When I Think of Pulse, I Think of Shakti," *QED: A Journal of GLBTQ Worldmaking* 3, no. 3 (2016): 111–13, 112, 113.

Conclusion

1 See Sara Ahmed, "White Men," *feministkilljoys* (blog), November 4, 2014, https://feministkilljoys.com/2014/11/04/white-men; and Ahmed, *Living a Feminist Life* (Durham, NC: Duke University Press, 2017), 15.
2 Alison Kafer, *Feminist, Queer, Crip* (Bloomington: Indiana University Press, 2013), 42–44.
3 Kai Cheng Thom, "This Trans Woman Never Felt 'Born in the Wrong Body'—And Here's Why That's So Beautiful," *Everyday Feminism*, July 26, 2015, https://everydayfeminism.com/2015/07/not-born-in-the-wrong-body.
4 Ed Sheeran, "Shape of You," on ÷ (London: Asylum UK/Atlantic UK, 2017); Sam Hunt, "Body like a Back Road," on *Body like a Back Road* (Nashville: MCA, 2017).
5 Mary Ann Saunders, direct message to the author on Facebook, June 29, 2018.
6 Conversation, July 14, 2018, Portland, Maine.
7 Prince and the Revolution, "Nothing Compares 2 U (OFFICIAL VERSION)," YouTube video, posted April 19, 2018, https://www.youtube.com/watch?time_continue=11&v=cpGAoazFdCs.
8 Caroline Palmer, "Dancers Recall Prince as a Hard-Working 'Darling' in Tights and Ballet Slippers," *Minneapolis Star Tribune*, May 5, 2016.

Afterword

1 Renee Gladman, Indexing Open Space, workshop presented at the symposium the Soup Is On: Experiment in Critical Practice, University of Chicago, June 1–2, 2018.

index

French Open, 32
Friedan, Betty, 88
"fucked-up shit," 18

Garcia, Angela, 99
García Bernal, Gael, 100
Geller, Pamela, 102, 104
gender categories, binary: Bunker on
    enemy formation and, 110; cisgen-
    der sexual dimorphism, 90–92;
    cis-skeletal privilege and, 102;
    denaturalization of, 31; messy and
    contextual boundaries, 70; non-
    consensual gendering, 95; physical
    and material evidence for classifica-
    tion, 94; political consequences of,
    106. *See also* death and cis-skeletal
    gendering presumptions on US-
    Mexico border
gender expression: "elective" vs. "es-
    sential" in, 59; hips and, 1, 21; spec-
    tating consensual gender, 57–60;
    stock habits as limiting, 62
gender identity: class reunion website
    and, 104; coloniality and, 94; as
    found and made, 64; gender at-
    tribution unconfirmed by, 94; mis-
    matches and, 8; Operation Stream-
    line and judicial presumptions
    of, 95; *Stone Butch Blues* and, 60;
    "wrong body" and "invisible me"
    discourses, 41, 112. *See also* death
    and cis-skeletal gendering presump-
    tions on US-Mexico border
gender-nonconforming people: *chicas
    trans*, 100; hips, boundary policing,
    and vulnerability, 9; "Latinx" and,
    93–94; legibility and, 101; outsides
    showing/hiding insides and, 11;
    Pride events and, 38
gender self-determination: access and
    barriers to, 18, 22, 58–60, 111; race
    and, 9–11; sexism, racism, and lan-
    guage of, 30–31
Gere, Cathy, 102
Gladman, Renee, 115
Glasson, Grace, 86–87

Godfather, The (Puzo), 72–76
Gomez, Jewelle, 58
Gossett, Che, 12
Gourdine, Angeletta K. M., 20–21
Gray, Mary, 64
Green, Kai M., 30, 89

Hacker, Marilyn, 48, 50–51, 58
hairstyles, 53–56
Hall, John S., 90
Hall, Radclyffe, 52
Hames-García, Michael, 106–7
Hamill, Dorothy, 54–55
Haritaworn, Jin, 59
Heathers (film), 78, 80–81
He Mele a Hilo: A Hilo Song (Aoki), 66, 68
Hersh, Kody, 94
Her Tongue on My Theory (Kiss and
    Tell), 86
hiding: as always racialized, 42; decep-
    tion, characterizations of, 11, 42;
    evasiveness, 56; of hips or curves,
    5, 8; in Kiss and Tell's *Her Tongue
    on My Theory*, 86; outsides hiding
    or showing insides, 11, 27; Tide ad
    and, 45; trans people and suspicions
    of, 42. *See also* insides/outsides
    disjunctures
high school reunion websites, 103–4
hip checks: external forces and, 115;
    as inspection, flirtation, or sports
    move, 2–3, 13; as off-balancing, 13;
    by own body, 16–17, 111–13; as power
    move, 104; sports rule books and,
    23–25; in writing, 67–68, 109; of
    your own writing, 115–17
hip opening, 17, 61–62
hips: about, 1–2; as bone, 8; boundary
    policing and vulnerability, 9; "boy-
    ish," 25; cis-skeletal privilege and,
    12; as lateral protrusions, 24–25; loss
    of, 16–17, 41; size of, 25–26; who has
    them, 23–25
HIV/AIDS, 77, 79
hockey, 23
HRC Corporate Equality Index, 35, 38
hula hoops, 62–63, 65–66

templates, gender binary in, 103–5

tennis, 30–33

"This Trans Woman Never Felt 'Born in the Wrong Body'—And Here's Why That's So Beautiful" (Thom), 112

Thom, Kai Cheng, 112

Thomas, Debi, 28–30, 54

Tide Super Bowl ad, 42–46

Tohono O'odham people, 97

Transparent (Amazon), 43–45

trans people and representation: characterizations and discourses, 41–42; *chicas trans* identity, 100–101; cis-trans binary, 12, 70; in *The Fosters* episode, 46–47; legibility and, 101; "man in a dress" trope, 44; Tide Super Bowl ad, 42–46; "tipping point" in visibility, 42, 44; "wrong body" discourse, 41, 112

trans window advertising, 43–44

US-Mexico border deaths. *See* death and cis-skeletal gendering presumptions on US-Mexico border

vaginas, 73–76, 87

visibility: evasiveness and, 56; in Feinberg's *Stone Butch Blues*, 59; "invisible me" discourse, 41; strategies of, 101; tipping point and, 44; trans people and, 41–42

Well of Loneliness, The (Hall), 52

"Whatta Man" (Salt-N-Pepa), 92

"When I Think of Pulse, I Think of Shakti" (Hames-García), 106–7

"When Something Is Not Right" (Aoki), 82–84

White, Anne, 32

White, Melissa Autumn, 98

whiteness, 10–12, 53–56

white saviorism, 69

white supremacy: anatomical racial hierarchies and, 20; Burger King Proud Whopper campaign and, 36–37; LGBT movement and, 10, 39; writing and, 15, 50. *See also* race, racism, and racialization

Who Is Dayani Cristal? (documentary; Silver), 98, 100–102

Williams, Dell, 87

Williams, Serena, 30–33

Witt, Katerina, 28–30, 54

woman as category, racist exclusion from, 30

Women's Flat Track Derby Association (WFTDA), 24

Women's National Basketball Association (WNBA), 24–25

writing: another (s)way, finding, 16, 67–68, 71, 109; binary-destabilizing language and, 30–31; Bunker's six principles of "post-binary writing," 109–10; editing out, 17–22; experimentation, 14–17, 115; hip-checking, intentionally, 115–17; sidelining and, 109; snark and, 50, 56; transferring oral narratives to text, 79; "WAIT, but!," 16, 67, 113–14; "writing as thinking" and "writing to learn," 111; "Yes, AND!," 113–14

Yohan, Dilcy, 98, 100–101

Zenobia July (Bunker), 109–10